RACE, CLASS, AND FAMILY INTERVENTION

Engaging Parents and Families for Academic Success

William Alfred Sampson

Rowman & Littlefield Education
Lanham, Maryland • Toronto • Plymouth, UK
2007

Published in the United States of America
by Rowman & Littlefield Education
A Division of Rowman & Littlefield Publishers, Inc.
A wholly owned subsidiary of The Rowman & Littlefield Publishing Group, Inc.
4501 Forbes Boulevard, Suite 200, Lanham, Maryland 20706
www.rowmaneducation.com

Estover Road
Plymouth PL6 7PY
United Kingdom

British Library Cataloguing in Publication Information Available

Library of Congress Cataloging-in-Publication Data

Sampson, William A., 1946–
  Race, class, and family intervention : engaging parents and families for
academic success / William Alfred Sampson.
    p. cm.
  Includes bibliographical references and index.
  ISBN-13: 978-1-57886-628-1 (hardcover : alk. paper)
  ISBN-13: 978-1-57886-629-8 (pbk. : alk. paper)
  ISBN-10: 1-57886-628-6 (hardcover : alk. paper)
  ISBN-10: 1-57886-629-4 (pbk. : alk. paper)
  1. Home and school—United States—Case studies. 2. Education—Parent
participation—United States—Case studies. 3. Minorities—Education—
Social aspects—United States—Case studies. I. Title.
  LC225.3.S33 2007
  371.19'2—dc22   2007005564

⊗™ The paper used in this publication meets the minimum requirements
of American National Standard for Information Sciences—Permanence of
Paper for Printed Library Materials, ANSI/NISO Z39.48-1992.
Manufactured in the United States of America.

CONTENTS

PREFACE

I continue to believe that family is the key to improved academic performance when it comes to poor nonwhite students. This is not intended to suggest that schools and school-based variables, especially class size and preschool education, are not important. However, the research linking family values, beliefs, and specific behaviors to the academic success of those students suggests a powerful link between family interaction and the academic performance of poor nonwhite children.

I have suggested in talks with family-centered practitioners and with colleagues that the actor Bill Cosby was probably right to suggest that many poor black families need to change the household dynamic if they want to help the children perform better in school and in life. We have a fairly clear idea of the variables in the homes of academically successful poor nonwhite students that are associated with good school performance. Thus, it made sense to determine whether it was possible to alter the household dynamics of poor black and poor Latino families that have underachieving students in a way and to a degree that would help them better prepare their children for a comparable educational experience.

This kind of ethnographic research is not easy. It involved locating poor black and poor Latino parents who had children who were not doing very well in school and convincing them to allow us to observe the families for months. We then spent many months more trying to teach them how to change their behavior, their attitudes, and, indeed, their values to more closely resemble those typically found in the homes of middle-class, though not necessarily middle-income, homes. We were in and out of the homes of these families for almost a year and a half—a very long time to so closely observe and work with poor families that often have better things to do.

As I have discussed, my research has centered upon discovering why some poor nonwhite families have students doing well in school while others in the same neighborhoods, who are equally poor, have children attending the same schools who often are underachievers. People have often asked me what should be done about the findings. This is a diffi-cult question for me given that I am a scholar and not a practitioner. I see my role as doing the research that answers the question of why some and not others, and I leave it to the practitioners to determine just what, if anything, to do with that data.

Of course, there are some scholars such as Epstein and Comer who have worked in both worlds, but I prefer to try to keep the lines between research and practice as clear as I can. This is not always easy when one sees poor nonwhite children who might be able to do better in school if their parents could and would change some very important things at home.

ACKNOWLEDGMENTS

Obviously, I could not do this work on my own. I could not even gain the access to the poor nonwhite families that was essential for the research by myself. I thank the staff members of the three Family Focus sites involved with this research not only for helping with the access but, more importantly, for helping to design and implement the curricula that were used to try to determine whether we could effect the needed family changes. Thank you, Nora Hernandez, Connie Sierra, JoAnn Avery, Sheree Davis, Wayne Lee, and Celita Jamison, who oversaw the project for the central Family Focus office.

I also thank the DePaul University students who observed the families twice for this effort: Nichole Long, Ian Petchenik, Robert Vargas, Johnathon Pierce, Brenda Salgado, Rosa Ramirez, Juana Telles, Taylor Yeftich, Julie Courtney, Ryan Dunigan, Mike Urbanus, Suzee Bending, Justin McMillan, Adriana Romero, and Esmeralda Martinez. Finally, I thank Angela Johnson for her advice and encouragement throughout this process.

INTRODUCTION

According to Irving (1990), "There is a strong relationship among black student achievement, teen parenthood, and poverty. Poor black students usually score lower on standardized measures of achievement and are overrepresented in the ranks of dropouts and pregnant girls" (p. xiv). James Comer tells us, "Students in our nation's inner cities underachieve and drop out of school at alarming rates. They are often more than two grade levels behind in Language Arts and Mathematics by the fourth grade" (1993, p. 300). There has been for years little doubt that poor nonwhite students in our schools, including suburban schools, do significantly worse in terms of academic achievement than do their white counterparts. The variables involved—race, social class, and achievement—evoke strong responses in America, a nation ostensibly devoted to equality and excellence. While I am concerned about the performance gap and its implications, my major concern for this work is not with the gap between black students (more precisely, poor black students) and white (more precisely, middle-income white students), but with the performance of only poor Latino and poor black students.

This is my focus because like Clark (1983) I have found that some poor Latino and some poor black students do well in school while others do not. Students from the same poor neighborhoods attending the same schools have very different levels of achievement. This fact is ignored because the focus has been upon the gap between the larger group of blacks and whites, and because few have bothered to look in detail at the performances of poor blacks to see that some of them do well. The overall data suggests that "they" perform poorly, but this data camouflages the achievement of some. If, however, some poor blacks and some poor Latinos can do well in school (most do not), then it may be possible for others to do well too, since neither poverty nor race explains the differences. Furthermore, if it is in fact the very low performance of poor blacks and poor Latinos that is responsible for a large part of the gap between blacks generally and Latinos generally and whites, then it would make sense in terms of educational policy to try to improve the performance of those at the bottom of the distribution. Not all poor Latinos or poor blacks are at that position. Again, my focus is not the gap between blacks and whites, or Latinos and whites, but between poor Latinos and poor Latinos and poor blacks and poor blacks.

The question for most others has not been whether black, and now Latino, students fail to perform in school at the same level as do white students. No, there is no doubt about that. The question is why, and whether this is the case for all or most black or Latino students. Another question is the role of what appears to be social class. Irving, in the first sentence of the above quotation, makes no distinction between black students and poor black students, while Comer specifically refers to "inner city" students, who are likely to be both poor and nonwhite. At times, scholars, policy makers, and concerned parents write or talk about the performance gap in racial terms alone, and at other times the focus is upon poor nonwhites.

The reality is that black students do not do as well in school as do white students, *and* that poor black students do even worse. The discussion about the performance gap should be more specific than is often the case, but this is sometimes difficult considering that even middle-income black students often perform significantly worse than whites in school. It is important for policy purposes, however, to know whether we are discussing all black, and increasingly Latino, students, or whether we are focusing upon poor nonwhite students. Are we to concentrate our efforts upon those at the bottom of the distribution, poor nonwhites, or upon all black, and many Latino, students? While I have elected in my research (Sampson, 2002, 2003, 2004) to focus upon poor black and poor Latino students and their families, others have been less specific and have therefore only served to muddle the discussion.

In his 1978 book, John Ogbu discusses the achievement gap between "blacks and whites." In his 2003 book, he writes, "We set out to discover some of the reasons for the low school performance of Black students in the Shaker Heights schools" (p. xiii). Given that Shaker Heights, Ohio, is a solidly middle-income community, it may have made sense to focus upon all black students, and given that in his 1978 book he is concerned with the broader issues of race, education, and caste, the broader focus makes sense. However, to use the terms *black* and *poor black* interchangeably is a mistake with policy implications. Are we to try to improve the performance of all black students, or are we to try to improve the performance of poor black students? Both approaches are warranted, but it makes more sense to me to concentrate upon those at the bottom, perhaps those who most need the help.

I need to point out here that my focus has been upon both poor blacks and poor Latinos, despite the reality that almost all of the research on the educational achievement of nonwhites has centered upon only blacks. So, on occasion it is tricky to write about the performance gap when most other scholars are writing about blacks only and I must therefore add Latinos to the discussion. I do this because increasingly our inner-city neighborhoods are the home of poor blacks and poor Latinos and the schools there are serving these people. The discussion of the performance gap must be expanded to include these Latino students, many of whom are also faring poorly.

Notice that I qualify the above statement. I am not falling into the trap of suggesting that all poor Latino or all poor black students perform poorly. Howell and Peterson (2002) for example write, "The differences in the test scores of blacks and whites have deep roots" (p. 3).

This of course suggests that all blacks are the same when in fact they are not. Many are poor to be certain, but many are middle-income as well. The middle-income or, as Ogbu (2003) and others refer to them, "middle class" blacks perform better than do poor blacks (and poor Latinos), but not as well as whites. Many poor nonwhite students do quite well in school, even schools that themselves have problems. This fact goes for the most part unnoticed and is not mentioned in the discussion about how to deal with the gap. Efforts to narrow or eliminate this difference in academic performance between poor blacks and poor Latinos and whites must, however, recognize this reality.

Reginald Clark (1983) recognized this more than 30 years ago, as has Janine Bempechat (1998) and Jean Murphy (2003). In my studies (Sampson, 2003, 2004), we observed poor black and poor Latino students who performed well above average in school as well as those who did poorly in the classroom. The question for me was not whether some could do well, but why them and not others? This is an important question for policy makers, for if we can answer it, then perhaps we can use that information to help improve the performance of the underachievers.

EXPLAINING THE GAP

But why the gap? Why is it that poor black and poor Latino students do worse in school than (middle-class) whites? There are of course a number of explanations for the difference. Jensen (1969) and Herrnstein and Murray (1994) suggest that the difference in performance for blacks is a function of their lower IQ. Ogbu (2003), however, persuasively debunks this argument. There is little to suggest that significant differences in IQ between poor blacks and poor Latinos socialized in the United States are the cause of the differences in performance (see Bempechat, 1998).

Howell and Peterson (2002) appear to attribute the gap to the legacy of slavery and discrimination. There is little doubt that school segregation is an important cause of poor school performance (Mickelson, 1998). However, I have studied poor blacks (and Latinos) who live in the same community, have family incomes that are about the same, attend the same schools, and are sometimes in the same classrooms, yet have significant differences in school performance. So, school segregation could not explain the difference because even among blacks and Latinos there was none. Admittedly, it is quite possible that segregation might have helped to explain differences in performance between whites and poor blacks and poor Latinos, but I did not study this. My focus has been and continues to be the explanation of the differences in performance among poor Latinos and poor blacks. I have no doubt that segregation may help explain the gap, but my concentration has not been upon the gap between whites and nonwhites, but upon the gap between some poor blacks and Latinos and other poor blacks and Latinos.

There are of course a number of other explanations for the difference in performance between blacks and whites. Irving (1990) argues that teacher expectations and cultural differences between blacks and whites are the primary factors. Ogbu (2003) discusses both explanations and, although not rejecting them, finds them both inadequate. There is of course the social class explanation. That is, blacks do not perform as well as whites because of significant differences in social class. The argument is generally based upon comparisons between poor blacks and middle-income whites, and the data indicates that the (poor) black students do not do as well as the (middle-income) whites. It is also true, however, that middle-income blacks do not do as well as middle-income whites, although they do better than poor blacks (Ogbu, 2003).

The social class argument, while sometimes strained due to the incorrect comparisons, is a fairly strong one. However, it is not particularly important for my work given that I am concerned only with performances among poor blacks and Latinos. Still, there is a dimension of social class, which is important for my work. Public schools are middle-class institutions both in their organization and management (Comer, 1993), and in their expected outcomes. As Comer writes, "The school is an instrument of the mainstream culture" (p. 305). By "mainstream," he appears to mean "middle class." Schools stress characteristics such as discipline and the ability to delay gratification. They stress responsibility and internal control. These are all generally seen as mainstream or middle-class characteristics. Furthermore, public schools are expected to produce citizens who will take their place among the middle class of our society. They produce teachers and customer service workers, firefighters and social workers, and they are charged by society with ensuring that the potential workers have the required knowledge, skills, and behavior shaped by values to play these roles.

However, *middle class* and *middle income* are not the same despite that even most scholars who study social class use the terms interchangeably. For most scholars of social stratification, social class typically involves some combination of education, occupation, income, and in some cases race. Middle-class folks are then seen as having some combination of these variables, which place them near the distribution of these variables. It makes more sense not to focus upon these easily measurable variables when discussing social class, but upon the values, beliefs, and behaviors that might be associated with the variables. It makes little sense to discuss social class without discussing the behavioral implications of class, and behavior is influenced by several things, including, perhaps most important, values, beliefs, and opportunity.

The problem with this approach is that values, beliefs, and behavior are difficult to measure and time consuming as well. So, we measure education, occupation, and income instead when what we really want to know is how these variables influence behavior. Clark (1983) found that the high-achieving poor black students whom he studied had parents who were calm with them and expected the children to play a major role in their own education. They had high educational expectations, established specific status structures with themselves as the authority, and established firm and consistent rules. They also provided nurturance and support for the high achievers. I have found that parents of poor Latino and poor black students who do well in school work to develop in their children high self-esteem as well as the ability to delay gratification, to show discipline and a sense of responsibility, and to focus upon the future. The parents spend a great deal of time with the children and are supportive and calm. The higher achievers also have parents who help with schoolwork and maintain a quiet, orderly home environment (Sampson, 2002, 2004).

To a significant degree these are characteristics generally associated with the middle class, or the mainstream, as Comer (1993) puts it. They are also characteristics highly prized in public schools, so there should be little surprise that students with these characteristics often do well in school. If, however, they are characteristics of poor children who also do well in school, what then? In my conceptualization these are middle-class poor folks who manage despite often horrific and daunting obstacles to have values and beliefs that shape their behavior and the rearing of their children in such a way that the children often do quite well in school. There is no achievement gap for these students. We should not be surprised to find that many middle-class students perform well in a middle-class institution. The surprise for some is that some of these higher achievers are poor and nonwhite. I believe that they are middle-class and lower-income folks without the opportunity to demonstrate their "middle-classness" in other ways given the limitations of their circumstances.

In a still-debated speech to mark the fiftieth anniversary of the historic *Brown v. Board of Education* decision, actor Bill Cosby suggested that "lower economic people" are "not parenting," and public scholar Dr. Michael Eric Dyson quickly took him to task. Indeed, Dr. Dyson had his book, which is quite critical of Mr. Cosby, published the very next year. Mr. Cosby was both right and wrong. Many poor black parents do not maintain the quiet, orderly home environment that Clark (1983), myself (2002, 2004), and others, including Comer (1993), have found to be associated with higher achievement among poor nonwhites. Some do the necessary things in the home to send their children prepared for the learning experience, and for the most part their children do well in school. By using such a broad brush, Cosby shortchanges some poor blacks.

Dr. Dyson is, however, guilty of the same offense and, as a scholar, he should know better. He refers to Mr. Cosby's words as "bile," and goes on to point out that Mr. Cosby "slights the economic, social, political and other structural barriers that poor black parents are up against" (2005, 70). Research, including my own, suggests that some poor black (and Latino as well) parents do indeed overcome these barriers to send their children to school prepared to learn, while others cannot. These barriers are not permanent obstacles to the success of some poor black and Latino students, though they certainly are for many. In this context, Cosby's suggestion that these barriers should be overcome makes some sense, because some overcome them. On the other hand, the data does make it clear that most poor blacks need help to overcome them. Furthermore, our society needs to help in this process if we are to be true to our guiding principles. Dyson ignores those who do not overcome them, and Cosby ignores those who do.

CURRENT RESEARCH

I have been aware through anecdotal evidence over the years that some poor black students living in poor neighborhoods and attending schools in those neighborhoods do quite well in school. Five years ago I decided to employ ethnographic methods to determine precisely why some poor black students do well academically while others do not. I had trained observers visit the homes of 12 poor black families living in the same neighborhoods, with their children attending the same schools for 2 months. The observers listened and watched for hours a week over that 2-month time period. This approach, while similar to Clark's (1983) and to that used by Lareau (2000), was a much deeper effort. While I also had the parents and children interviewed as did Clark and Lareau, I used very detailed and long-term observations of the entire family dynamic as the main source of my data. Both Clark and Lareau used interviews and short-term observations.

Being in the homes for weeks at a time allowed me to determine in greater detail what parents did and said consistently that influenced the school performance of their children. I compared the report cards of the 12 students and then compared the home–family dynamic of those who did well in school with those who did poorly or average to determine the precise role of the family in school preparation. This approach begins with the assumption, informed by previous research (Clark, 1983; Entwisle, Alexander, & Olson, 1997; Murphy, 2003; Tapia, 2000; Trueba, 1988), that the family plays a major role in the school preparation and academic success of children, and perhaps particularly poor children. This approach in a sense holds constant race, income, neighborhood, and school-based factors (6 of the 12 students observed attended one school, while 3 other attended another school). So, it is highly unlikely that race, social class (as generally defined), neighborhood, or teacher training had much to do with the performance of these students.

I disagree with Irving (1990) that the different "cultural characteristics" of many low-income black students has much impact on performance. If that were the case, it would be unlikely that 6 of the 12 students I observed in my first work on this topic (Sampson, 2002) would have been high achievers. For they were all low-income black students living in the same neighborhood and presumably sharing the same cultural characteristics. Still, some did well in school while others who were in many ways much like them did poorly. There was, however, one critical way in which they differed, and that is in what did and did not happen in the home. While almost all of the parents express a great deal of support for and have fairly high expectations of education, the home environment and approach to school preparation differed significantly between the high- and average-achieving students and the low achievers.

The average and high achievers have homes that were quiet, orderly, and highly structured. Much of the talking in these homes centered on school activities. These students were involved in extracurricular activities, which promote and support discipline and responsibility. The parents (who were in most cases single parents, by the way) not only discuss schoolwork with the children, but very often attempted to help with the work, even when the work was beyond their ability. It was not the help that was important to the success of the students but the message about the importance of that work that the attention and help sent to the children. The average and high achievers had household chores that also taught discipline and responsibility, and they went right to either their chores or their homework when they arrived home from school. There was no television or video games for these students. Their parents complimented them on jobs well done and expected all work to be well done. So, these children had high self-esteem and high expectations, and their parents were almost always calm and supportive. These students expressed their expectation that they would attend college (they were middle-school students, by the way), and were internally controlled.

All of the characteristics listed are characteristics highly prized in public schools, and were present to some degree in 9 of the 12 households observed. I used the same approach with a total of 30 poor Latino and poor black families in the same—racially and economically—community (Evanston, Illinois) in two subsequent studies (Sampson, 2003, 2004) and had basically the same findings. While there were some significant differences among some Latino families related to language and gender role, for the most part we saw the same characteristics among the higher-achieving students and their families in the later work as was the case in the earlier research.

Given that these findings are close to those of Clark (1983), Bempechat (1998), Tapia (2000), and others who have studied school achievement as it relates to the family and home, I believe that we have now developed a fairly clear picture of what happens in the homes of poor black students who do well in school. We now have a good idea about what *needs* to happen in the homes of other poor Latino and poor black families if they are to have children perform well in school.

Yes, I am suggesting that we seriously consider intervention in the family lives of poor nonwhite students in an effort to help them perform better in school. A growing body of research has shown us that the family dynamic and approach to education and to preparing children for that education is different for those who have children who do well in school. Furthermore, we are able to see just what those differences are. I reasoned that it was time to test an intervention strategy based upon this knowledge. Some may discount this approach as blaming the victim and an attempt to "help" that victim. However, the data clearly indicates that some poor nonwhite families prepare their children for educational success while others do not. My data does not permit me to deal with the critical question of why some and not others. I can, however, lay out a strategy for the educational success of poor nonwhite families who elect to learn what they need to do to enhance the prospects for the educational success of their children.

I am not blaming the families at all. I have clearly seen that many poor nonwhite families face extraordinarily difficult conditions. We have observed families struggling with drug problems, families trying to deal with no money to pay the utility bills, and families without a man to serve as a male role model. We have seen mothers who must work full-time and still prepare their children for the learning experience on their own. Still, some of these families manage to send their children to school prepared to learn, and those students do very well.

The question I pose here is whether we can use this data to help other poor nonwhite families adequately prepare their children for that learning experience. I have seen that some poor nonwhite parents overcome poverty, race, and ethnicity, as well as the low expectations of our society to send their children to school prepared to learn. All other things being equal, those children do very well in school. Now, can we teach other poor nonwhite parents to do the same? Can we successfully shift the focus from the school to the home? Remember, the schools have been far less than successful in raising the level of performance of significant numbers of poor nonwhite students—thus, the continuing discussion of the performance gap.

After lengthy discussion with the leaders of Family Focus, a family-centered community agency in the Chicago area, we decided to ask a number of poor black and Latino families with young children in Chicago schools and Evanston (a Chicago suburb) schools who were known to do poorly to allow us to observe the families over 2 months. The data from those observations would be used to fashion a training curriculum to help parents better prepare their child for school. The children were all third- and fourth-graders. We wanted to find out whether we could utilize the data on what the parents of some poor non-white students did "wrong," as determined by previous research, and what some parents "right" to help the former better prepare their children. We measured the effects of the intervention by changes in grades and teacher evaluations over time, and by changes in the home environment and family dynamic.

Furstenberg et al. (1999) wrote, "A focus on success under unfavorable conditions can provide useful clues about which public policies could be adopted to assist children and families to cope with these conditions, thereby reducing the handicaps imposed on those economically disadvantaged at birth" (p. 6). The goal in my earlier work was to determine the precise role played by families in fashioning educational success among poor nonwhites. In this research, the goal was to determine whether we could use those earlier findings to train poor nonwhite parents to do the things done in the homes of academically successful poor nonwhite students. We also wanted to see whether our efforts resulted in significant improvements in the academic lives of the children studied and in the family dynamic of the families trained.

If we can train poor families to do those things done in the homes of successful poor children, then it may be time for policy makers to begin to shift their focus from only school-based solutions to solutions based in homes and with families. I am not suggesting that we ignore efforts to reduce class size or to provide more and better preschool education, because we know that such efforts have had a positive impact upon the academic performance of children, especially poor children. I am suggesting that a focus upon such "solutions" as vouchers or charter schools shows little indication of being successful for significant numbers of poor nonwhite students, and that any effort to raise the performance of the poor should include family-centered approaches. Tapia (2000), Ford

(1993), Sampson (2002, 2004), Murphy (2003), Ogbu (2003), Lareau (2000), Comer (1993), and Clark (1983) have all made this clear. The question that I posed for the current research was whether such a family-centered approach could actually improve performance. I wanted to put that focus to a test, to give policy makers more evidence that a shift in the location of school improvement efforts may make sense.

Part I

RACE, CLASS, AND EDUCATIONAL ACHIEVEMENT

RESEARCH METHODS

Research that involves spending hours at a time over months in the homes of families is time consuming and sometimes nerve wracking for both the researchers and the families. This is especially the case when the families are poor and might believe they have things that they would rather their neighbors not know. Many poor folks distrust, often with good reason, authority and intervention in their lives. Clark (1983) made this clear when he realized that he could not use school-based folks to gain entry into the homes of the 12 poor families that he studied. As I knew this from Clark's work, I have from the beginning asked Family Focus to help me to gain that entry. Family Focus works with hundreds of poor nonwhite families in the Chicago area in an effort to help them improve the quality of their lives, and many of those families trust the Family Focus staff, who work very closely with them.

In the past, I approached the staff members at the Family Focus facility in Evanston—the racially, ethnically, and economically diverse suburb just north of Chicago—and asked that they request dozens of poor black and poor Latino families to allow observers into their homes for 6 to 8 weeks. The parents were told that they were selected to participate in studies that the researchers hoped would shed light on the practices used by poor nonwhite families to help their children do better in school, and that this effort would probably not help them, but that it may help others like them. This study seeks to determine whether we can in fact help others in similar situations, and while I have long thought that this kind of research naturally followed the earlier work, the initial idea for the research came from the staff at Family Focus.

The idea was to select a number of poor children in both Evanston and Chicago, both black and Latino who were known to do poorly in school, and ask them to allow observers into their homes for several weeks so that we could determine what, if any, changes were needed in what parents did and did not do to prepare their children for school. Then I would analyze those observations to suggest to the staff at the three Family Focus sites involved in the research the design of a curriculum for change for each family. Selected staff members would then devote 4 months to the training of the parents, and, finally, we would reobserve the families to determine the extent to which positive changes had occurred in the homes that might be attributable to the intervention and training.

Near the end of the 4-month training period, the staff asked that the training be extended another 4 months, and I agreed to a 3-month extension. Thus, we trained the families involved in the research for a total of about 7 months. I will point out right away that educational policy makers will not normally have 7 months to train parents to better prepare their children for school. They will not often have the access to the homes that we had, and they may not have enough trained staff that have developed the necessary rapport with and trust of the poor families most in need of the intervention. So, even if the data suggests that this family-centered approach makes a difference in school, we need to be aware of the limitations of our approach. On the other hand, if the data suggests that this works, then perhaps policy makers need to consider modifying the approach to fit their time and economic constraints. If it works, some version of it needs to be seriously considered.

We began with four poor Latino families, one of which had two children being observed, two poor black families in one of the poorest and most violent neighborhoods in Chicago, and three poor families living in a historically black, and increasingly poor, neighborhood in Evanston. After the initial observations that took place in the fall of 2004, one of the Latino families refused to participate further, and one of the poor black families in Evanston moved from the state. Thus, we trained for some 7 months two poor black families in Evanston, three poor Latino families (with four children as the focus of the work) in a poor Chicago neighborhood, and two poor black families in a very poor Chicago neighborhood. The training followed almost 2 months of observation, and was followed by two more months of reobservation. We were therefore in the homes of seven poor Latino and poor black families for a year and a half!

It is almost unheard of in social science for researchers to spend this kind of time and go into this kind of depth with poor nonwhites. When observers visited the homes they stayed for 2 to 4 hours at a time, listening, watching, and later writing down everything that they could remember they saw and heard. It was then up to me to interpret and analyze those observations. They were trained to try to avoid any involvement with the families that might alter that which would "normally" happen were they not there. Obviously, this is very difficult, and is one of the reasons why they visited over months. While young children, and even parents, may "put on a show" for strangers for a time, it is highly unlikely that they can maintain this over several weeks.

In addition to the observations, we interviewed both the parents and the students in their homes. The interviews were used to gather baseline data about the families, to ascertain the parents' and children's views and expectations about education, and to help determine behavioral patterns related to the educational process. The ethnographic approach used for this research is not perfect, but I believe is much better suited for the kind of questions I posed than either survey research or retrospective research. This method is, however, very time consuming and can wear on the observers, particularly when they are observing people who may be struggling to meet basic needs. This generally means that the samples will be small, which limits generalizability, and therefore we need to see more of this kind of research in order to gain more confidence in the results (Lareau, 2000).

THE SAMPLE

As I have indicated above, I asked Family Focus staff to ask a number of poor Latino and poor black families with whom they regularly worked to agree to participate in a year long study. This study was designed to determine the degree to which parental behavior could be changed in order to help improve the educational achievement levels of a child in their home. Each of the three Family Focus centers then invited the families to meet with myself and trained observers at the respective Family Focus centers. The children were to be third- or fourth-graders who were doing poorly in school. I indicated to the Family Focus staff that I wanted to observe young children who had grades below C or, as in the case of Evanston—which does not give letter grades to students until the sixth grade—children whose achievement reports indicated they were below average in many areas.

I focused on younger students in the belief that if improvements were to occur they were most likely to occur for younger students. As Comer (1993) tells us, "Early school success at a reasonable level promotes the competence, confidence, and self-esteem needed for continued overall development and later school success" (p. 305). I believe that the earlier this success comes, the better the chances for overall academic success. The sooner students see themselves as academically capable and the sooner teachers and other school personnel see them as capable, the more likely it is that they will be successful overall. The sooner a child is prepared for the learning experience, the better the chances of academic success. The sooner they develop self-esteem, an ability to delay gratification, internal control, discipline, a sense of responsibility, study habits, and high educational expectations, the better the chances of doing well in school.

The observers were introduced to the parents and the students at the meetings, and arranged the first of what were to be a number of visits to the homes. As I have indicated, there were initially four Latino families living near the Family Focus site in the Chicago neighborhood called Hermosa, or the nearby neighborhood of Humboldt Park, both of which are heavily Latino neighborhoods, three poor black families in a poor and largely black area of Evanston, and two poor black families living in the Chicago neighborhood of North Lawndale. After one Latino family left the study and one black family moved from Evanston, we had three poor Latino families and four poor black families. In the case of one of the poor Latino families, the mother requested that we observe two brothers, 8 and 9 years old, and I agreed to do so. We ended up working with three poor Latino families (and four students) and four black families. The observations lasted for about 7 weeks, and generally lasted from 2 to 3 hours. Given that we were very interested in a number of aspects of the family dynamic as this related to schools, we generally observed the families after school and during the week, when it was more likely that school-related activities would have taken place.

The Hermosa neighborhood is 18.8% Latino, while the area in which Family Focus is located is 66.4% Latino. Almost 27% of the residents of Hermosa receive food stamps, 15.8% are below the poverty line, and 66.6% of the residents of the zip code area in which Hermosa is located speak a language other than English. Only 25.3% of the residents of Hermosa are high school graduates, and 32.5% of the residents of the area around the Family Focus site are foreign born.

The North Lawndale area in which the other Chicago Family Focus site is located is 93.5% black, and 70.2% of the children in the neighborhood receive food stamps. Only 29.4% of the residents of North Lawndale are high school graduates, and 40.7% are below the poverty line.

Evanston is, however, a much more diverse community than either of these two. It is home to Northwestern University as well as the national headquarters for several nonprofit operations. There are a number of wealthy folks, and the community leaders love to point out the large and gracious homes, and to point out that the school system is supposed to be one of the best in the nation. However, for the 2005 academic year, 4.5% of the white eighth-grade students in Evanston were below standards or worse in science on the Illinois Standards Achievement Test, compared with 40% of black eighth-graders and 32% of the Latino students.

In reading, the numbers were 4.9% for whites, 38.6% for blacks, and 44.3% for Latinos. In math, they were 9.5% for whites, 50% for blacks, and 47.2% for Latinos. So, while Evanston is economically, racially, and ethnically diverse, it is also the case that blacks and Latinos there are disproportionately poor, and that the black and Latino students fare considerably worse than do white students on the state standardized achievement test. Residents of Evanston are 5.3% below the poverty line, compared with 14.3% in the area served by Family Focus. That area is 82% black, while the city is 18.1% black. Almost

93% of the residents of the city are high school graduates, while 72.9% of the residents of the neighborhood around the Family Focus site are high school graduates. The seven families studied live in poor communities that have a disproportionate number of residents of the one race and ethnic group studied.

Guided by the work of Clark (1983), Tapia (2000), Lareau (2000), and my earlier work (Sampson, 2002, 2003, 2004) the observations and interviews focused upon family structure, family processes, the home environment, values and attitudes, and finally, educational processes. The goal was not to determine if what went on in the home affected school performance, because we already know that it does. Furthermore, we are developing a very clear picture of just what about the home and family affects school performance, and how. In this case, we used the data from the initial observations and answers from the questionnaires to help Family Focus staff develop a curriculum for each family that would be used to try to change—to improve, if you will—those processes, values, and behavior that we already know influence the academic performance of children. Thus, the initial observations and answers to the questionnaires were used as baseline data to help fashion the approach to each family so as to help the parents change what they did or did not do that influenced the school performance of their child (or in the one case, children).

This information was also used to help measure those changes. We observed the families a second time just over a year after the initial observations in an effort to determine the degree to which the intervention changed the processes, environment, values, and attitudes. I am well aware that a variety of things could influence those processes, values, attitudes, and environment. Family dynamics are generally not static, and this is probably especially the case for the poor, who must constantly adapt to circumstances and changes in their lives with minimal resources. Thus, we need to be careful to remember that this is not a controlled experiment, and that we do not have control over many of the things that might affect my conclusions. Still, if there are significant changes in the processes, values, and home environment, and/or in the performance of the students that might be attributable to the training, this will suggest not only that policy makers may want to consider this type of family-centered approach to improving the school performance of poor Latino and poor black students, but also that more research like this should be done. The sample is small, the work very time consuming and draining, and the children sufficiently young that variables other than my intervention may affect them.

The changes in performance were therefore not the only way in which I measured the impact of the training. I reobserved the families in part because of my belief that while other things could affect grades and reports from teachers, and improvements in performance may well take place over a longer time frame than was available to me, positive changes in the home environment and family dynamic might well occur sooner, and were used in this study as a second measure of positive impacts. I therefore measured change not only by changes in grades and school reports, but also by changes in the home that might at some point affect those grades and reports, and may be more likely to be the results of the training given that the training centered upon changing that family dynamic.

THE TRAINING

The training of each of the seven families involved in the research was based upon a curriculum developed by the staff at each of the three Family Focus sites working with the families. That curriculum was itself based upon the analysis of the first set of observations and centered on the family variables known to positively influence the school performance of poor nonwhite students. These include the following:

- *Family processes*: amount of interaction, type of interaction, parental intervention, discipline, responsibilities, and division of labor
- *Home environment*: space, noise, study arrangements, facilities within the home, books
- *Values and attitudes*: self-esteem, importance of education, importance of self-control, expectations, and ability to delay gratification
- *Educational processes*: homework arrangements, role of the parents(s) in the schoolwork of the child, value of education to the child and parent, grades of the child.

If, for example, the initial observations showed that a particular family did little to help a child develop positive self-esteem, or to maintain a home environment conducive to study and homework, then the curriculum for that family would focus upon helping the parent or parents understand the importance of these values/characteristics in school preparation, and to show the parent just how to develop the positive self-esteem and to maintain the home environment needed. Another family may already maintain the quiet, orderly, structured home environment that previous research shows is related to better school performance among poor Latino and poor black students.

The curriculum development process began in January of 2005, lasted approximately 1 month, and was then followed by 6 to 7 months of training, which took place both in the homes of the children and at the Family Focus sites. In the case of one Latino parent, for example, the curriculum and the training were to focus upon exploring the possibility that the student's homework assignments could be in Spanish to allow the parent to help with that homework, to help the parent develop strategies to better communicate with the teacher, to investigate possible after-school activities for the student, to identify easy-to-accomplish household chores to allow the student to take responsibility, and to help the family practice complimenting each other to help build self-esteem in addition to other important issues and activities.

The curriculum for one of the black families indicated that the family would be helped to identify a quiet, organized, well-lighted space for homework. The students would be encouraged to do homework in 30-minute intervals, and an area of the house that had no radio or television distractions would be identified as the area for homework. The child would be helped to develop an academic journal and the family would be referred to a nonprofit agency for counseling. This is of course not the entire curriculum, but it serves as an example of the types of issues that the staff members working with the analysis and with the families thought were important to focus on. It also demonstrates that the different families were seen to have different needs.

The reference to the need to refer a family for counseling is one reminder of the complexity involved with working closely with poor families. At one of the meetings I held with staff members involved with the research to discuss progress, one staff member mentioned that she was

working with a family with 11 children (and two parents) living in a one-
bedroom apartment. There is no practical way for that family to have the
kind of quiet, orderly, structured, home environment associated with
higher achievement among poor nonwhites. The parents have issues
that they must address daily, which, I am certain, come before the need
to work with the children on schoolwork. Indeed, one of the children
did not want to attend school because he could not wash regularly before school.

Another parent lost her job during the study and apparently turned to
alcohol. These issues must be addressed at least along with, and probably before, a parent can pay much attention to the preparation of their
child for the educational experience. Despite these obstacles, many
poor nonwhite parents manage to do many of the things that we know
are conducive to higher school achievement. In the case of this research
I wanted to determine whether we could help others to do the same.

2

INITIAL OBSERVATIONS

Kendra Allen is a 10-year-old fourth-grader at an Academy in Lawndale. In the third grading period of 2003, she received a D grade on the Chicago Reading Initiative, a D in writing standards, an F in listening, a D in speaking, a D in research methods, an F in math standards, a D in science, and a D in social science. She also had Ds and Fs in art, physical education, and library science. Clearly, Kendra was a very poor student, and she acknowledges that she is not doing "so well" in school. She suggests that she gets into trouble in school, suggesting perhaps some behavioral issues as well. Indeed, her teacher suggests that she needs to improve in following direction, working independently, coming to school prepared, completing homework, and showing respect for herself and others. It appears then that Kendra is not only a poor student but also has a number of the behavioral problems that will often get in the way of academic success.

In fact, it is these kinds of behavioral issues that will cause a teacher to see a student as difficult or a troublemaker, and then devote less than the needed time and energy in teaching that student. In this type of situation, the teacher is then seen as a poor teacher, when in reality the situation is not that simple.

Kendra believes that education is very important because it will help her obtain a job, and she wants to go to college. She reports that she devotes about 20 minutes a day to her homework, that she receives lots of help from her parent with her homework, and that she wants to get rich.

Her mother is a 30-year-old single mother with five children who was on leave from her job (she was 9 months pregnant). However, she indicated that she last worked 2 years ago. Ms. Allen completed high school, and thinks that Kendra's education is "very important." She encourages her by telling her to do her homework, to work harder, and to listen better and talk less. She says that she visits Kendra's school "twice a week," and indicates that Kendra is sometimes in trouble at the school, which makes sense given her behavioral report.

The observer noted that during the first visit, Kendra had trouble understanding a few of the questions from the questionnaire. Ms. Allen indicated during that visit that she takes parenting classes at Family Focus. Two of Kendra's siblings asked for sodas, and Ms. Allen told them to go to the kitchen to get them, and to get juice for the 1-year-old's bottle as well. They did as they were told, and also got candy and other snacks. When Ms. Allen realized that the boys had not gotten the juice, she told one of them to go back to the kitchen to get the juice. After about 5 minutes he had not returned with the juice, and Ms. Allen and her adult cousin joked that he was probably drinking the juice himself. Kendra was sent to check, and found that her brother was in fact drinking his sister's juice.

Ms. Allen yelled to the boy to come back or else she would "pop him in the jaw." He still did not come back for a time, and Ms. Allen indicated that he knew that given her pregnancy she could not get off the sofa to pop him. This suggests that her method of discipline is physical, and that the children may well push her to force the discipline. However, when she told the boys to take their shoes to their room and to put on their house shoes, they ran off. Kendra did as she was told. Kendra indicated that she wanted to be a Girl Scout, but Ms. Allen said "no way." She refuses to sell cookies or to be Den Mother. She does not appear to be prepared to support her daughter's involvement in this extracurricular activity that helps to build discipline, self-esteem, and a sense of responsibility. Kendra has no interest in other extracurricular activities, according to her. When asked what she did all day, Kendra replied that she stared at the walls, to which her mother replied that this was the truth. This does not suggest that she does much schoolwork, or that her mother helps her or guides her. She is apparently allowed to do nothing.

Ms. Allen indicated that she feels that her neighborhood is so unsafe that the children are not allowed outside unless she is with them. When Kendra was told to change the baby's diaper, she did so right away. The boys were told to prepare their dinner, and then Kendra was told to make hamburgers. They all did as they were told. Kendra told the observer that she had written in her diary that her mother was fat, and that when Ms. Allen discovered this she took away her radio for a week. Ms. Allen seems to discipline the children, but it is not clear how effective this is.

During the next visit, Kendra was again observed doing as she was told, this time by an adult who was not her mother. The television was on in the backroom, and Kendra asked the observer to help her with her math. After a few minutes of math work, she read an old English text (with help) for a few minutes. Later Ms. Allen told her to make a bottle for the newborn. When the bottle leaked, Kendra told her younger brother to clean the mess up, which he did.

During another visit, Kendra mentioned that she would not go to after-school reading anymore because she did not want to do so. Apparently Ms. Allen does nothing about this. Kendra also indicated that she had recently been "jumped" at her school, and that she wanted the school to close because she does not like it. Ms. Allen came into the room and told Kendra to put on her house shoes. She did not do so. Then Ms. Allen told the observer that Kendra had been expelled from after-school reading because she had refused to take her coat off, and that she was going to "beat the living mess out of her" after the observer left. She explained that Kendra had a bad attitude. She does not appear to know just what to do about this though.

When the boys arrived, their mother told them to clean up the mess in their room. Ms. Allen informed the observer that Kendra had recently pretended to be ill to avoid attending school, but that she had made her go. A bit later the boys, along with two other boys, went outside, only to run back to tell their mother that one of them was beaten by another boy. Ms. Allen ran outside to confront the offender, who told her that he had hit the son because he had given him "attitude." The boys were told again to clean up their room when they went back inside.

Later Kendra and a girlfriend talked about schoolwork, but did none of it, while the boys played loudly. Kendra told the observer that other children and teachers try to prevent her from doing well in school (she did not say this for the questionnaire), but she did not believe that her mother would be supportive, so she said nothing to her. Fordham and Ogbu (1986), among others, have made the point that there exists among some minority students a desire to see other students who are members of those groups do poorly in school, and resulting pressure to bring this about. However, such pressure is far more likely to occur when some of the students are doing well and others poorly. Clearly, Kendra is not doing well in school, so it is not clear why anyone would pressure her to do poorly.

For the first time, Kendra was observed doing schoolwork during the fourth visit. This was done, however, in the living room while the observer and Ms. Allen talked, an environment not particularly conducive to schoolwork. Apparently Kendra had gotten into trouble in school again. This time she had walked out of class. According to her, two boys threw crayons at her, so she walked out. Her mother believes that something else is going on. She also said that she planned to beat Kendra's teacher's "ass" whenever she saw her because she had not returned her calls about the incident. She has gotten into other fights with adults over the children according to her. The previous night the newborn slept with Kendra so that Ms. Allen could rest. When Kendra was told to prepare a bottle for the baby, she replied that she still had homework to complete. Ms. Allen, however, told her to make the bottle. So, the 10-year-old fourth-grader appears to be a caretaker for her newborn sibling.

The observer noted during the next visit that the house was a mess. There was garbage, toys, and paper all over the floors. Kendra ate dinner and watched the television in her room, before joining her brothers, a guest, and other children to watch the television and to play. No schoolwork was done, and there was a great deal of noise and confusion.

During the last visit, the observer was told about illicit activity on the part of relatives of the family, and that Ms. Allen might be pregnant again. Kendra tried to read to the observer, but often got stuck on words. When she did, she explained, she simply made up words. Ms. Allen told the observer that she was to visit Kendra's school the next day, and asked about her homework, only to be told that she has completed it in school.

There is little to indicate that this family has any of the characteristics of the poor families with children who perform well in school. While Ms. Allen tries to run a tight ship, the children do not respond to her until she threatens them. The house is disorganized, chaotic, and unstructured. There is noise almost all of the time, and almost no schoolwork is done. When it is, Ms. Allen plays no role. There is no effort to boost the self-esteem of Kendra. In fact, there were many instances of efforts to belittle the student, which lowers self-esteem. The only discussion of school has to do with Kendra getting into trouble, and Ms. Allen wanting to fight her teacher. There are no extracurricular activities, no assigned household chores, no real responsibility on the part of the student. So, we saw little discipline, no structure, no responsibility, little homework, and no help from the parent with that work, such as it was. Kendra does much of what she is told to do, though not always when she is told to do it. She shows little self-control, and must take on responsibilities that would seem to be beyond her years, if not beyond her capacity.

Almost none of the characteristics of high-achieving poor black students found by Clark (1983) or myself (Sampson, 2002, 2004) were present in this home. Ms. Lewis is not calm with Kendra. She plays little role in her schooling, and may well play a negative role. There is frequent conflict in the home and minimal help with the little homework that Kendra tries to do. It is fairly clear that this student and her family need help if she is to become a better student. It is also clear, however, that conditions exist in the home and for the family that may make such changes quite difficult.

IDA SMITH

Ida Smith is a 10-year-old fifth-grader at an Academy in Lawndale, but not the same school attended by Kendra Allen. At the end of the 2004 school year, when she was a fourth-grader, her grades were as follows: a D in the Reading Initiative, a D in writing standards, a C in listening, a C in speaking standards, a D in research standards, a D in math, a C in science, and a D in social science. She received all Cs in her art, music, and physical education courses. Like Kendra she lives in Lawndale. Early in the 2004–2005 academic year, Ida had some behavioral problems according to her school report, including problems with self-control, accepting the guidance of the teacher, following rules and regulations, and showing respect for herself and others. However, by the end of the spring grading period in 2005, the only poor mark was in accepting the guidance of the teacher. I shall need to return to this issue later given that our intervention efforts began in the winter of 2005, which means that it is possible that the improvements were linked to that intervention.

When asked what she most liked about her school, Ida replied that it was the teachers and the after-school activities. She least likes her art class, and believes that she is doing fair in school. Education is "very important" to her, indeed, "more than anything in the world." This is a fairly strong affirmation of the value of education for a fifth-grader. Ida does report peer pressure to "ditch school." That is, she does feel that other students try to keep her from doing well in school, and that they do this because they do not value their education. Given her fairly low grades, this is difficult to understand. Peers do not normally try to hinder students who are doing poorly in school. On the other hand, this is a young lady who has seemingly managed to control her attitude and behavior problems, perhaps a student who is on the right track, despite the grades. It is possible, though I consider it unlikely, that Ida's grades are a reflection of this pressure.

Ida reports that she devotes 2 hours a day to her homework, she expects to attend college, and sees no obstacles in her way. School is the most important thing in her life, and according to her, her parents help with her schoolwork every time she does the work. She wants to be a teacher. So, the young lady appears to be very focused upon education.

Ms. Small, her adoptive mother, is 59 years old and is retired. Her husband works, and they both receive GEDs. She too believes that education is very important because it is needed to get a "decent job" and to allow one to "take care of self." She encourages Ida to do well in school by telling her how hard it is to get a good job without an education. Note that education is closely related to very practical (and particularly high) goals, and not for itself or for what it does in shaping the individual. This is often the case with poor folks, and is different from the case for many middle-income folks. She visits Ida's school three or four times a week, "if not everyday." This is a lot, and could be very good for Ida if it is true. This could be a plus because it suggests to Ida the value of education. At the school, Ms. Small helps with meetings, in the classroom, and is the chairperson for one of the organizations at school. A real plus. This type of involvement tells the student that education is so important that her parent takes the time to involve herself in it. Kendra gets no such message. Indeed, her mother was not involved in any way whatsoever.

Ms. Small also noted peer pressure upon Ida to skip school. She tries to teach Ida self-control, and to use punishments that are educational. It appears that this parent has some idea of what is required for good school performance. She values self-control, involves herself in school, and is aware of the attempts of other students to limit her child. These are some of the characteristics of higher-achieving students. Yet, Ida is not a high achiever.

Ida lives in a "neat" but small and cramped house in Lawndale, and lives with both parents. This is important because Ms. Small, given that she is retired, has the time to spend helping with the education of Ida. There were two other children in the home, both boys, during the first visit, but one does not appear to live there, and appears to belong to a daughter of Ms. Small. The television was on in two rooms the entire time of the first observation, including while Ida and her brother sat together doing homework. While it is positive that homework was being done, it is not positive that the television was on the entire time. That is a distraction. There was also no evidence that either parent helped with the homework or asked about it or school. After about 20 minutes with the homework, Ida complained that she was bored, and her father suggested that she read a Bible book, which she did, though the television was still on. So, reading is apparently important to Ida and her parents. This was not the case for Kendra or her mother. While Ida worked on her homework and read "softly," her brother worked on his homework. So, it does appear that schoolwork is valued in this home, though the parents do not seem to understand the importance of quiet. Ms. Small, her husband, and the woman who seems to be a daughter discussed No Child Left Behind and school activities, suggesting that they pay attention to school and to education. Very positive. But, the discussion was "loud" while the children worked on homework.

The next visit took place on a school holiday, but all of the older children present were working on homework when the observer arrived, though, again, the television was on. When a younger child began to distract Ida and the other child doing homework, Ms. Small "disciplined" that child, and the homework continued for another 40 minutes. So, Ida does devote a fair amount of time to homework, even on holidays, and her mother does seem to understand the importance of this work.

After eating, Ida again began to read while watching the television. For a time, a younger child made a lot of noise but "soon order was restored," and Ms. Small, who was watching another television, began to discuss the news with the children. She asked them about Yasser Arafat, who had died that day, and other questions about the news, suggesting that she expects them to keep up with the news and that they be prepared to answer questions about the news. This is very positive, because it suggests that she expects them to learn all of the time, and to be prepared to show that they have learned. This requires a sense of responsibility, discipline, and attention to detail.

During the next visit, the younger child was looking at his "words," which were flash cards, as Ida began her homework. When the younger child threw his cards into the air, Ms. Small demanded that he quiet down to allow Ida to do her homework. So, Ms. Small understands the value of quiet and order, and expects that homework will be done (though she does not seem to help with that work). The television is a distraction, however. After 20 minutes of homework/television, Ida again organized the papers in her book bag before going into the kitchen. Her father arrived later to find her lying on a couch watching the television, and asked, "Ida, don't you have a book you could be reading?" Again, reading is valued in this home, as is the discipline to do that reading as opposed to watching the television, though the latter is a fixture.

When the observer arrived for the next observation, Ida was again doing homework with the television on. I should note that Ms. Small had asked the observer for copies of both of my two books published at that time. The observer gave them to her during this visit. I mention this because it may be that Ms. Small is aware of what the academicians say is needed in the home if poor children are to do well in school, and suggests the concern of the parent with the education of the child.

Ida watched the television as she wrote a paper for school. After completing that paper she asked her mother to read it. Another indication of the importance of knowledge and the help of the parent to Ida. Ms. Small questioned Ida about her assignment, in fact, asking very specific questions about the paper before giving it back and suggesting that it needed more work. When Ida asked for more help she was told, "I can't write your paper for you." Ida then resumed work on her own, though the room was chaotic as the youngest child ran all over the room yelling loudly. Ms. Small eventually came to calm him down, briefly.

This family seems to have several of the characteristics found in the homes of high achievers. Ida consistently does her homework with occasional help from her mother. Her father wants her to read often. The house is not particularly quiet, but is normally structured and orderly. Ida's evenings are centered on schoolwork, and she is expected to think. Her mother involves herself in school activities that show Ida the value of education. Ms. Small, while tolerant, expects discipline, even from the 3-year-old, who is, by the way, working on his spelling and reading, and was at one point quizzed by Ida about a board game. The parents keep up with the news, and seem to expect that the older children will as well. Ida seems to be responsible and disciplined, and learning is valued in the home. Despite the fact that the family displays several of the characteristics of higher-achieving students, Ida is not doing well in school.

JASON GREEN

Jason is a 9-year-old fourth-grader at the middle school attended by most of the students from the neighborhood in which he lives in Evanston. While his behavior and work habits appear to be satisfactory, that is, his teacher reports no behavior problems, he was below grade level in three of the eight reading categories, four of the eight writing categories, five of the ten math categories, and one of the three science categories. He is clearly a below-average student.

Jason most likes his gym class, and least likes homework, suggesting not much focus on or perhaps interest in school. He believes that he is doing fair in school, and that education is important because "it helps you learn." It is not clear then that he has a sense of the value of education given that he says that it is important because of its definition. He was unclear about how much time he devotes to homework, but he wants to attend college. He sees no obstacles in his way, and his family is the most important thing in his life. Jason indicates that he receives help with his schoolwork from Family Focus, his mother, and his brother. If he could be any other person in the world, that person would be Kobe Bryant, the basketball star.

Ms. Green, Jason's mother, is 32 years old and has lived in Evanston all of her life. Like Ms. Allen, she is a single mother, has four children, and works as a file clerk. She received a certificate in business systems. Ms. Green believes that Jason's education is very important because "in society they think the black man should end up in jail, and if they don't have an education there is no job." Like many poor parents she equates education with a better job. She encourages her son to do well in school by telling him what a good job he has done when he does well, and letting him know that he can participate in sports if he does well. So, it seems that she is mindful of the need for high self-esteem, and the need to develop responsibility, given that she ties the participation in sports to school performance.

Ms. Green indicates that she cannot visit the school attended by Jason because she has to work. This is often a problem for poor single mothers. Their work schedule makes visits to the school problematic, and it is not necessarily the case that they do not want to visit the school. However, while many of the mothers whom we have observed say that they visit schools often, we have seen very little evidence to support this. When she does visit the school she is happy because the teachers apparently let Jason know "what a good child he is." Well, he may be "good," but he is not a good student. If teachers are telling her and him how "good" he is, they are focusing upon his good behavior and ignoring his poor performance. This would not be uncommon with poor nonwhite boys, a number of whom might pose behavioral problems and make life difficult for teachers. When one does not, the teachers may seem happy and satisfied. This is unacceptable on the part of the teachers if it means that they fail to push and support his academic efforts because they place him in a category with others whose behavior or attitude may mean more work for them.

She believes that it is important that black children be "praised, and told that they are doing a good job" in order to avoid feeling like a failure. Clearly, she sees the importance of high self-esteem, something that we have seen in the homes of poor nonwhite high achievers. The only obstacle to Jason's receiving a good education is money for tuition. Ms. Green is an only child and indicates that she is "a brat." She raises Jason to respect adults, and to show good manners. Based upon his behavior reports, this is successful. So, Ms. Green stresses high self-esteem, manners, respect, and perhaps responsibility. Jason's attitude, behavior, and self-esteem seem to be very much like the characteristics of higher achievers.

The observer described Jason as "quiet and extremely well behaved" during her first visit with him, which began at Family Focus. He was polite and followed direction well. He was "talkative but shy." Later the observer and Jason left Family Focus and went to Jason's apartment, which was described as "cold, dark," with "clothing everywhere." There were "piles of dirt everywhere." The one television is in Ms. Green's room, and there were "clothes and trash on stairs." The kitchen had "lots of dirty dishes covering the counters, kitchen table, and sink." I mention this description because it suggests something about the order, or lack thereof, of the home, and therefore the potential difficulty for Jason in doing his schoolwork at home. In fact, the observer noted that there was "nowhere to sit in the house." This would not be the ideal home environment in which to consistently do schoolwork.

When Ms. Green arrived, she sent Jason to the grocery to buy milk and potato chips. She then turned on music and drank a beer while cleaning the kitchen. When Jason returned he began to watch the television and to eat the chips. His mother later asked about his homework and whether he had practiced his musical instrument, and was told that he had done both at Family Focus, though the observer had not seen him do either. Ms. Green made no attempt to document that the homework was done and no effort to help or to look at the work. Jason seemed to like the attention paid by the observer, and there was no attention paid to schoolwork or school in the home.

The observer next met Jason at Family Focus at 4:15 p.m. When asked whether he had completed his homework, he replied that he had. If this was true, he did not devote much time to the work given that he had been out of school for a very short time. Jason told the observer that he had attended church on Sunday, that he sang in the church choir, and that he had played football over the weekend. These extracurricular activities help develop discipline and responsibility, and by all accounts, Jason is a disciplined and responsible young man. However, his home environment does not promote good academic performance and, so far, we have not seen his mother pay the kind of attention to his schoolwork that she needs to. The teacher in the room at Family Focus told the observer that Jason was a "great kid, always calm and well behaved." So, a foundation seems to be in place, but some aspects of good school preparation such as a quiet, orderly, structured home environment, and the importance of the schoolwork and the mother's involvement in that work were not in evidence.

The observer noted during the next visit (begun at Family Focus) that Jason likes to keep busy and is "very good with time management." He again indicated that he had completed his homework, and even offered to help the observer with her homework. He also told the observer how important it was to vote. He seems to be a thoughtful, well-behaved student. When dinnertime arrived, Jason volunteered to help serve the dinner.

When the two went to Jason's apartment the observer noted that it was not as messy or dirty as the last time, but was still cluttered. This visit was kept short at the request of Ms. Green, who had errands to run and, again, there was no mention of schoolwork or school.

Ms. Green did ask Jason about his homework during the next visit, which ended at the home of Jason's grandmother, but she did no more than ask whether the work was finished. For his part, Jason turned on a television, a computer, and a CD player, not the best environment for schoolwork. Jason asked the observer to read a piece of paper that turned out to be a school assignment, before Ms. Green asked to read the assignment as well. She said little about the reading assignment, but mentioned that Jason liked to read. While the younger children played,

Ms. Green completed the parental questionnaire herself, stopping several times to ask the observer how to spell different words. I should note that on a few occasions Jason also helped his mother with her spelling.

The observer noted during her next visit, which like the others began at Family Focus, that Jason asked to help the observer with her homework again. The young man is thoughtful. He indicated, yet again, that he had completed his homework, though we never saw him do any schoolwork, either at home or at Family Focus, and his mother never really paid any attention to that work, despite her obvious concern for and attention to Jason. On this occasion the observer noted that Jason "is very responsible" and that "he follows directions well." It appears that a number of the characteristics of successful students are in place here: discipline, responsibility, and high self-esteem. However, Ms. Green does not seem to pay enough direct attention to schoolwork or to school-related matters, and she does not require this of her son. The home environment needs work to be more conducive to schoolwork. At this point, since schoolwork is not a serious part of the life of the student, this is not an issue to Ms. Green.

After leaving Family Focus with Ms. Green, the observer and Jason were driven by a friend to the grandmother's home, where Jason began to watch the television right away. He then paged through a toy catalog while his mother read the mail and drank a beer. There was no schoolwork done, and no discussion of school. I would also note that while Jason is thoughtful and considerate, he was not observed doing any household chores consistently.

The student has the discipline and sense of responsibility, as well as the self-assurance seen in high-achieving poor black students. But, there is very little attention paid to school in his home, despite Ms. Green's professed interest in his education. I would note, however, that Ms. Green might assume that the work is being done at Family Focus. While this does not seem to be the case, even if it were, she should learn the value of following up on that work every single day, and maintain an environment in which that work can be done with her input. Given that she may not spell well, she may be sensitive to her involvement with the work. Some attention should also be paid to delayed gratification given that Jason does no schoolwork at home, preferring to play games and to watch the television and listen to music. Ms. Green is loving and caring, but does not translate these characteristics into the type of behavior that will help her son in school. However, the love, care, and attention to respect, responsibility, and self-esteem can serve as building blocks.

ANITA TERRY

Anita is a 10-year-old fifth-grader in Evanston. Her behavior and work habits were fine on her last report except that she needed to practice greater self-control and that she failed to always complete her class work on time. Anita needs an intervention plan to work at grade level in three of the seven reading categories, in three of the nine math categories, and three of the four science categories. Furthermore, she was not making satisfactory progress toward meeting grade-level standards in four of the nine math categories. She also needed some help in social studies, and a lot of help in history. By all accounts, Anita is a poor student with self-control problems, and she fails to complete her class work on time.

Anita likes her friends, reading, and the principal at her school, and she dislikes her teacher, who, according to Anita, yells at her. She does not like the boys because they call her ugly, and she thinks that math is boring, and does not like the fact that she gets poor grades in math. She believes that she is doing fair in school, which seems to be a bit of an exaggeration. Education is very important to Anita because she will "need it in life." According to her, she devotes about 20 minutes a day to homework, which seems like a very little amount of time, and she expects to go to college. Her family and her education are the most important things in her life. Anita indicates that her grandmother helps her with her homework if she does not complete the work at Family Focus. I have observed dozens of students at Family Focus now, and I have seen very few do much schoolwork there over the years. Anita may be an exception, but I doubt it.

If she could change one thing about her life it would be to start school over so that she could "get better at things" she is not good at. She wants to be a teacher.

Anita lives with her maternal grandmother, who has lived in Evanston for almost all of her 61 years. There is one other child in the home, Anita's 8-year-old sister, and the grandmother, Ms. Robbins, does not work. Ms. Robbins completed high school and nursing school, and believes that Anita's education is "very important" because it will help her become independent and allow her to take care of herself. This seems to be a rather low level of expectations. Ms. Robbins says that she encourages Anita to do well in school by buying her books, communicating with the school, and helping with her homework. She says that she picks Anita up from school daily, and attends conferences at the school. When she visits, she feels "anxious" because she sees a great deal of "chaos" at school. The kids are not learning the basics, according to Ms. Robbins. She believes that the students are too concerned with the "social aspects," and that this concern, along with her lack of money, limits the educational possibilities for Anita.

Interestingly, Ms. Robbins says that teachers, as well as the Evanston Board of Education, stand in Anita's way. She indicates that the Board does not allocate enough money for schools, that teachers need to improve their skills and to teach at different levels. So, she seems to pay attention to education, but it also appears that she blames everyone else for Anita's educational problems. At some point, it would seem that she must learn to deal with her responsibility, and that of her granddaughter. She mentions that race is a factor in her life, and it appears that Anita is biracial. She describes her upbringing as "confusing," and noted that her mother had married three times by the time Anita was in the sixth grade.

She wants Anita to feel "safe and secure" and "grounded," and to know how important education is. She criticizes the schools for having "lost touch," and being too busy trying to get the students out of the schools.

The observer first met with the family at Family Focus, and waited with a sister and Ms. Robbins until Anita returned from a field trip. The family lives in South Evanston, quite a distance from Family Focus, and the observer described their apartment as "pretty clean," "not spotless" but "not dirty either." Anita indicated that she had failed to complete her homework because of the field trip, before she changed clothes and began to play with her sister and turned on the television. The observer noted that Ms. Robbins was very quick to yell at the sisters. (She was quite stern with the younger sister while they waited at Family Focus as well.) However, she remained in the kitchen while the girls played in the living room. She asked Anita about her homework as she parked the car when they arrived, and the observer noted that she "pushed the ideas of homework," asking about it two times, but not asking to see the work or to help with the work. She asked that the television be turned off, but the girls turned it back on a few minutes later.

Anita had taken her homework out while the girls watched the television and played, devoting little time or attention to the work. Anita indicated that she is a cheerleader, which of course could be very good for discipline and a sense of responsibility. However, the children for the most part did as they pleased during this first visit, and they did not pay much attention to schoolwork at all.

The next visit also began at Family Focus, and Anita was not seen doing any work, though, to be fair, there was a Halloween party that day. The observer described the children as "loud, chaotic, and shouting." When Ms. Robbins walked into the room she showed the observer Anita's progress report from school, which indicated that Anita had no grade higher than a C, and had two failing grades. She indicated that she believed that either the school or Family Focus were not doing their job, but felt that it was more likely the school. She told the observer that she was going to the school the next day. Given that Ms. Robbins is at home she has the time to attend the school, and she appears to have the necessary concern. Again, though, she does not seem to consider her role in the educational process.

When they arrived at the apartment, the girls began to draw pictures and write while watching the television. Ms. Robbins never asked about school or homework, and for the second time no dinner had been served or mentioned when the observer left at almost 9 p.m. While Ms. Robbins had indicated that she picks Anita up from school daily, she was in fact seen to pick up Anita from Family Focus, from where all of the observations began.

When the observer arrived at Family Focus for the next observation she noted that students appeared to be doing homework. This is noteworthy because it has not often been the case. However, they were unruly during the blessing of the food given them by their adult supervisor. Anita indicated that she devotes about 5 minutes to her homework, but 10 minutes to her math. So, she does not seem to spend much time on schoolwork, and it does not appear thus far that her grandmother pays much attention to this. While seeming to do her homework, Anita drifted back and forth between the work and conversation with others, and the room was "loud." Not really conducive to homework. The observer wrote, "Anita seemed like she wanted to sit there and do her work, but she could not resist the temptations around her." Well, those temptations should not be there, and she should have the discipline to resist them.

During the ride home, Anita and her sister argued with and yelled at Ms. Robbins because she would not allow their friend to sleep over that evening. In fact, when they arrived at the friend's home to drop her off, Ms. Robbins had to lock the back door so that they would not jump out of the car. Anita told her grandmother that "[she] is mean and that she hates her." It is clear that discipline is an issue here. When they arrived home, they watched the television, a movie, and worked on Anita's hair. There was no homework done, Ms. Robbins did not ask about homework or school, and no household chores were done either. The environment was not conducive to homework in any event.

The next visit also began at Family Focus, and the room was again chaotic and noisy, with two groups of girls dancing to music in different parts of the room. Ms. Robbins arrived earlier than usual, explaining to the observer that Anita's social worker was visiting that day. During the ride home, Ms. Robbins yelled at the girls "a few times, but nothing close to the usual." When they arrived at the apartment, the girls got snacks and turned the television on, something they seem to do every evening.

When the social worker arrived, she told Anita to turn the television off and began to ask her about several things, including boyfriends and grades. Anita told her that she had gotten grades of 100 on everything that week, but there was no evidence of this. The social worker asked whether she had received help with that work from her grandmother or Family Focus, to which Anita replied no, that she is "just smart." This suggests both that Anita has a distorted sense of her own academic standing and that her grandmother is not nearly as involved with her school life as she needs to be. When asked why she believed that, she replied, "Because I just do." So, there may well be self-esteem issues here as well. I should note that Anita's mother was involved in a very traumatic event that also involved

Anita's younger brother, which Anita witnessed. While I do not want to make too much of this at this point, it must be noted and the reality is that this may well have an impact upon her academic success at this point in her life.

The social worker indicated that a recent assessment of Anita indicated that she has trouble concentrating, and that she has dreams that relive a traumatic experience. Later, Anita complained about the adult supervisor at Family Focus because she "concentrates too much on homework," and does not allow enough playtime. So, she does not seem to want to do homework, was not seen doing much of it, and has no one paying much attention to this at all. She displayed a lot of anger this evening toward her sister.

There were more observations, but the picture is fairly clear. Ms. Robbins is rather distant and yells at the children all of the time. She pays very little attention to what goes on in school or at Family Focus, and needs to learn the use of and approaches to discipline. Anita is not at all focused on school. The house is noisy and there is little structure at home. Anita has discipline issues, anger issues, and self-esteem issues. Furthermore, she has witnessed a very traumatic event, and this must be kept in mind in dealing with her. Anita and her sister prepare their own food, usually junk food, eat when they please, and do pretty much as they please. Despite her answers to the questionnaire indicating her value of education, Ms. Robbins did nothing to suggest either that she really has that value or that she knows what to do about it. Just about the entire list of issues for families in which a student is doing poorly is here. Plus, there is that traumatic event. Unfortunately, these types of events are not that uncommon in the lives of the poor.

JUAN LUIS MARTIENEZ

Juan Luis is a 9-year-old currently in the third grade who received a D in writing standards, a D in listening, a C in speaking, a D+ in math, a D− in science, and a D in social science. He also needed help with his self-control, making independent decisions, being courteous to others, and completing tasks successfully. So, in addition to his academic problems, Juan Luis has some behavioral problems as well. He says that he likes everything about his school, and thinks that he is doing well, suggesting either that he does not really understand what doing well is or that he is willing to settle for poor performance.

Juan Luis thinks that his education is important to him "because he learns," and he says that he devotes 20 minutes a day to his homework. He wants to go to college, and his only obstacle is getting into a fight. His family is most important to him, and he gets "a lot" of help from family with his schoolwork. In fact, according to Juan Luis, he receives this help even when he does not need it. If this is true, it is a good sign.

Juan Luis lives with his 51-year-old grandmother, Ms. Tajeda, who is the fiancée of the head of the house. She has lived in Chicago for 35 years (but spoke Spanish), and is from Puerto Rico. There are three other children living in the house, but unlike many of the poor black families observed, and like most of the Latino families observed, this family has two adults present. This should allow more time for at least one of them to attend to the child. Ms. Tajeda does not work, giving her the time mentioned. Her fiancé completed 2 years of college, while Ms. Tajeda completed 2 years of high school.

Juan Luis's education is very important to Ms. Tajeda because she wants "the best" for him; she wants him to become someone in life. She tries to encourage Juan Luis by "talking to him, explaining and helping him." She attends his school often; she "is always there." In fact, she is a member of the local school council. When she is at the school she is confident, but says that sometimes she feels "out of place." This is sometimes a problem for poor parents because schools and teachers can be intimidating. If they are, it is more difficult to help parents because they need to work with schools to help their children do well. On occasion, schools that have a number of poor students seem to forget this, making life more difficult for the parents of these students.

Ms. Tajeda believes that Juan Luis was limited in his educational progress by "his mother's situation." Juan Luis was apparently placed with Ms. Tajeda by the Department of Children and Family Services, and according to her she makes certain that "he does all of his school things first." She believes that other children limit Juan Luis by encouraging him to play and avoid homework. Her own parents were strict with her, and she moved around a great deal, going to different family members and friends. In raising Juan Luis she stresses discipline, and she relies upon herself when she has a problem. I should note that Ms. Tajeda is the paternal grandmother, and Juan Luis's mother, according to Ms. Tajeda, failed to feed her children or to pay rent due to illness. Ms. Tajeda has also adopted two of her sister's children, a 14-year-old and a 16-year-old.

During the first observation, Juan Luis informed the observer that he had completed his homework and that he pays attention to what his grandmother tells him to do, though he misses his mother. Juan Luis watched the television and told the observer that he does not do much. He did not that day, and Ms. Tajeda did not ask about school or require him to do anything around the house. However, during the next visit, Ms. Tajeda asked Juan Luis about a science project, which he explained to her while on the way home from school. Juan Luis's teacher had told Ms. Tajeda that he had failed to turn the project in. She also asked about other homework assignments, and Juan Luis replied that he had one left to do. When they arrived at the apartment, she asked to see the science project. I should note that Juan Luis speaks only English, but Ms. Tajeda completed the questionnaire and the consent forms in Spanish. She might well have trouble helping with homework that is in English, though she does speak limited English.

Juan Luis colored and drew until Ms. Tajeda began to try to teach him his times tables, which he had trouble understanding, and this frustrated Ms. Tajeda. She soon gave up. A friend of Juan Luis had come to get him to play, but Ms. Tajeda told the friend that Juan was busy. Juan Luis, however, told the friend to wait in another place and he would be out to play. After he left to find the friend, the boyfriend/fiancé of Ms. Tajeda went to get him explaining that he could not go outside because he was being punished for something that had happened the day before. Juan Luis cried and went to his room. The boyfriend entered the room, asked a question, which Juan Luis did not answer, and told Juan Luis that he was now being punished for two more days. Juan Luis had a few minutes earlier told his grandmother that he did not like the boyfriend. So, the male whom Juan Luis does not like is involved with punishment, which Juan Luis apparently does not like either, and Ms. Tajeda seems to accept this situation. Having him in the home frees her up from working and allows more time with the children, but she does not seem to know how to use that time wisely.

Ms. Tajeda does ask about schoolwork, but it is not clear how much she can help given the language issue. Discipline seems to be an issue as well. Juan Luis ended up going outside anyway once the boyfriend left and his grandmother was using the telephone. He went to buy chips and juice. His grandmother finally found him and asked why he would buy juice and chips when there was so much food in the house and she had prepared dinner. Juan Luis told her that he did not want that food.

As soon as Juan Luis arrived home during the next observation, he went to his room and turned on the television to play a video game. Ms. Tajeda asked about his homework and told him to turn the game off. He ignored her. She continued to implore him to do the work and he admitted to the observer that he had a lot of work to do. For a brief time, Juan Luis turned his attention to the homework and then yelled that it was complete. Ms. Tajeda asked an older sister to check the work, and the sister confirmed that it was correct. He returned to the television.

During the next visit Juan Luis and his brother were cleaning their room, and Ms. Tajeda, after some time, told Juan Luis to do his homework, only to have him respond that it was complete. Later he began to listen to CDs, and to play fight with his brother before going to the kitchen to make a sandwich. There was no work done, no discussion of school or that work, no quiet time, no evidence of responsibility. In fact we saw little evidence of any of these characteristics during our visits. Ms. Tajeda seems to want very badly for Juan Luis to do well and is apparently willing to help. However, she does not know what to do, and allows Juan Luis to do pretty much as he pleases. There is no attention to schoolwork or helping with that work, none to self-esteem, none to keeping the home quiet, none to internal control, and little to delayed gratification. Juan Luis does no assigned household chores (he is young, but not so young that he does not go around the neighborhood alone), and we see no evidence of any responsibility. His grandmother's desire to have him do well is a positive, and she seems prepared to do her part, once she knows that part.

I have found in the past (Sampson, 2003) patterns very much like this one with other poor Latino families: a parent very much wants to help a student to do better in school, but is stymied by the language issue and by a lack of knowledge of just what to do to better prepare the student. The will is often there, but the knowledge is not. In most cases with

Latino families, there is a father and a mother in the home, which allows the female to stay at home, even though the family is poor. This gives that female more time and energy to devote to school preparation, but it will not matter much if she does not know what to do or is limited by an inability to speak English or by an insensitivity to this limitation on the part of school personnel.

JOSE ROSALES

Jose is an 8-year-old third-grader who attends the same school as Juan Luis, and most likes his homework and the after-school program. This is different for a student who is not doing so well, though Jose is doing better than some of the other students involved in this research. His grades were mostly Cs and Ds at the end of the 2003–2004 academic year. For the fall grading period during which we observed his family, he had Ds in reading and writing, a C in listening, a C in math, an A in science, and a B in social science, suggesting that he is becoming an average student. His teacher did indicate that he needs improvement in several language arts categories, especially writing, one math category, and in work and social habits categories. So, he does better than most in this study, but clearly could do better.

He least likes being yelled at when caught running in the halls of the school. Jose thinks that he is doing well in school, but believes that his mother thinks that he is doing fair, suggesting perhaps that she would like for him to do better. If this is the case, it is a positive. School is important to him because he wants to learn and to study. Again, an unusual answer for a young student who could perform better in school. He says that one student bothers him in class, that he is a bully, and he sees this as an attempt to keep him from doing well in school.

"Not doing bad things" is most important to Jose, and he says that "everyone" helps him with his schoolwork "everyday." This suggests that he receives a great deal of help with his schoolwork at home, and, if true, is very positive. If he could change one thing about his family life, it would be the behavior of his aunt, who he says fights a lot.

His mother, Ms. Roman, is a 27-year-old single mother, works as a cashier at a fast-food restaurant, and grew up in Mexico. There are three adults living in the apartment, along with two children. Ms. Roman completed the 11th grade, and said that Jose's education means "too much" to her because she wants him to be "superior," to surpass her. She tries to encourage Jose to do well in school by mentioning various role models to him, so that "he could grow up to be great like them," suggesting that she has high expectations for Jose. Ms. Roman visits Jose's school once a week and feels both happy and worried when she visits. She is happy because she knows that he will advance if she becomes involved, and is worried that he will fail. She likes to ask his teacher about Jose. It does appear that she has the desire to do the things required of her in order for Jose to be properly prepared for the educational experience and, in fact, she sees nothing standing in his way. She does point out, however, that Jose has gotten into trouble for talking during class. This suggests that Jose may have both a discipline and a delay-of-gratification problem, both of which are likely to limit academic success.

Ms. Roman indicates that her home life was both happy and "not happy." Her father never hit her, but her mother sometimes did. She wants to raise Jose differently, disciplining him "in a good way." This appears to suggest that she does not want to use physical discipline. She reads a book a few minutes a day when she has the chance, and relies upon her sister when she has a problem.

The observer described Jose's apartment as "nice and tidy," though she noted that there were a number of roaches in the living room. He has a 3-year-old brother who is cared for by his grandmother when Ms. Roman is working. During this visit, Ms. Roman explained that Jose's father was incarcerated when Jose began school, and this, in her view, had affected Jose negatively because he "was" close to his father. As a result she had Jose see a therapist to get the help that she believed he needed. This sounds like a thoughtful, concerned mother. She noted that since they moved and Jose had changed schools he did not receive as much homework, and she noted that she had been told that because he was doing poorly in school he might be held back a year.

She talked with his teachers and as a result Jose began (that day) to attend an after-school reading program 3 days a week. Again, Ms. Roman shows her concern for Jose's education and her willingness to do that which she realizes needs to be done to be helpful, much like many middle-class mothers, though this mother is clearly quite poor.

When the observer arrived for the next observation, Jose was "ready to start his homework." Ms. Roman asked him what work he needed to do. The 3-year-old brother was a distraction, and Ms. Roman wanted to take him into another room so that Jose would have no distraction. While Jose worked on his assignment a man entered and at one point asked whether Jose needed any help. Jose identified the man as his father, but remember that Ms. Roman indicated that she is single. Jose did not complete the work by the time that the observer prepared to leave, and no one checked on this.

The apartment was described as tidier and quieter by the observer when she arrived for the next visit. The television was on but Ms. Roman asked Jose to turn it off and he complied right away. There was no homework done this time, and much of the time was devoted to completing the questionnaires, which took a fair amount of time because both Ms. Roman and Jose had difficulty understanding some of the questions, which were asked in Spanish.

The observer described Jose as polite, and he seems to be very respectful as well. During the next visit, he asked his mother whether he could watch the television. This is very different from the situation with many of the students observed, who simply turn on the television when they arrive home, and often fail to turn it off even when asked to do so by a parent. Ms. Roman suggested that he draw rather than watch the television, and he began to do as he was told. Ms. Roman told the observer that Jose had a project that required him to select five different countries, determine the foods eaten in those countries for the holidays (Thanksgiving and Christmas), and then show pictures of those foods. Ms. Roman indicated that she knew what the foods were for Mexico and Puerto Rico but wondered about America. She asked the observer to write the American foods down for her. She said that she planned to cut out pictures of those foods and then to have Jose write the foods down using the pictures so that he could communicate the material to his classmates. Clearly Ms. Roman wants to help prepare Jose for school, and she is willing to do what she must to help him do better. Language and culture appear to be problems for her, but she is prepared to be involved. She is also raising a disciplined, respectful young man, though he apparently has problems with the discipline at school on occasion.

Jose continued his drawing as Ms. Roman commented that this was what he should be doing rather than watching the television. I should note that during this time the younger brother constantly interrupted Jose. When the brother demanded to use Jose's notebook and pen, Jose refused. Ms. Roman asked Jose to allow this and to use a different notebook, and while Jose complied, he was clearly upset by this. He became very quiet and withdrawn, and his mother told the observer that this was the way he often acted. He then began to work on a maze in an activity book and Ms. Roman soon asked to see this work as well, commenting that he had inappropriately crossed over a line. She pays a fair amount of attention to what he does, but we have not seen him do a great deal of schoolwork, despite the fact that he has difficulty with both reading and writing.

We observed no evidence of involvement in extracurricular activities or efforts to ensure high self-esteem or responsibility. However, the house is fairly conducive to schoolwork (though the younger brother can create distractions), and the apartment could be quieter when Jose is at home after school. Ms. Roman is willing to do what she needs to do in order to help Jose perform better. Jose shows discipline at home, though he can get away with sulking when he does not get his way. Ms. Roman is receptive to things that might help, and on several occasions asked the observer for suggestions concerning both Jose and her. It appears that she needs to learn the value of high self-esteem, a more conducive home environment (the live-in grandmother could help more with the 3-year-old), responsibility, and internal control. She needs to understand that Jose should do schoolwork or reading and writing, which will help him in school everyday, and that she should ask about this and help with the work consistently. This is not currently done, but she appears to be willing. Again, however, if the work comes home in English, her ability to involve herself with the work would be limited.

FEDERICO AND JOSE LUIS VILLAR

In an unusual situation we observed two students from the same family at the same time, Federico and Jose Luis Villar, both of whom attend the same school attended by two other Latino students observed. Federico is a 9-year-old fourth-grader, while his brother Jose Luis is an 8-year-old third-grader. At the end of the 2003–2004 academic year Federico's grades were mostly Cs and Bs, which indicates that he was doing somewhat better than several other students involved in this research. His teacher indicated early that year that he needed improvement in some work habits, but that was apparently not a problem in the last marking period, the period before our observations. His brother, Jose Luis, received a B− in Spanish, a C− in math, and B− grades in science and social science. He did not need improvement in any habits or attitudes. Both students were in English as a Second Language (ESL) programs, and Jose Luis received C and C− grades in reading, listening, and speaking in that program. His brother received two C grades and one B. I would say that these are average students and not the low achievers that we sought and that we have seen thus far. They can do better, however, and we at the request of the parent tried to help her to better prepare the students for school in an effort to determine whether that help would improve their performances.

Jose Luis received grades of C−, B+, C, D+, C+, and C in the main academic areas, and a D, a C, a B, and a C in his ESL curriculum at the start of the 2004–2005 academic years, that is, during the time of our initial observations. Federico received mainly B and C grades at the start of our observations, and his teacher thought that he needed improvement completing his assigned class and homework. Again, neither student seems to have serious attitude or behavioral problems and both are doing fairly well in school.

Their mother, Norma, believes, however, that they are both doing poorly in school and need help to do better. Federico most likes lunch, gym, music, and pizza about school, and Jose Luis most likes the principal. So, neither likes anything academic about school. They both least like reading, and Jose Luis adds math to that list. So, they dislike the main academic areas. Neither believes that education is very important, and Jose Luis thinks that he is doing pretty well while Federico thinks that he is doing good in school. I believe that these may be the first students I have observed who believe that education is not important. If they cannot see the value of education, there is no reason for them to even try to do well. Their parents are essentially responsible for imparting that value, and they must be made to understand this and to learn just how to do it.

Education is not important to Jose Luis because he becomes bored with school, and Federico believes that he could be taught better in another school. Each brother believes that others have tried to prevent him from doing well, and they both blame others for talking to them, which they believe makes them misbehave. It sounds like they are not accepting the responsibility for their actions, for young people will talk with others when they should not, but students must learn to do the right things in any case. Neither knows why other students bother them. Federico says that he devotes an hour a day to his schoolwork, while Jose Luis spends half an hour on his work. They each would like to go to high school, indicating very low educational expectations, and Jose Luis actually expects to go to the fifth grade while his brother expects to get as far as the eighth grade. These expectations must rise, and the parents must be taught how to help in this process. It would be easy to think that the students did not understand the questions, and perhaps they did not. However, other students their age did understand them, and if these two did not then their level of understanding appears to be low. For Jose Luis, his family is the most important thing in his life, while grades are most important for Federico, a strange answer given his low educational expectations and his apparent dislike of academics.

Federico indicates that he receives "a lot" of help with his schoolwork from his parents, while Jose Luis receives help "occasionally," whenever he asks for help, and sometimes they help "for no reason." If it is true that they help when he does not ask, this would be positive, for it suggests concern on their part for his education. While they both believe that the help provided is "enough," Jose Luis indicated that he would like a little more help when the observer followed the question with another. If he could change one thing about his family life, Federico would have a larger television and better carpeting, while Jose Luis would behave better, an indication of behavioral problems but also of his awareness of them. If they could be any one person, Federico would be himself, perhaps suggesting self-confidence, and his brother would be the President so that he could stop the war in Iraq, an astute position for an 8-year-old.

The mother of the boys, Ms. Sanchez, is 49 years old, married, and has lived in Chicago for 18 years. She is from Mexico, and lives with seven of her children. Her husband collects scrap to sell at junkyards. He never attended school, while she completed the 12th grade. Ms. Sanchez believes that the education of her sons is important because she does not want them to join gangs. So, at this point she does not seem to expect too much of them, though gangs can be a very serious issue. These expectations, or what Ford (1993) refers to as "achievement orientation," have a positive impact upon student achievement. In this case both the expectations of the mother and those of the students are quite low.

Ms. Sanchez tries to encourage her sons to do well by helping with homework, and by giving them "little presents" when they do well. So, she says that she helps with schoolwork and does things to boost self-esteem, both of which are very positive if done consistently. She visits their school every week, and feels good because she is told positive things about the boys when at school. I would note that she indicated that the teachers with whom she speaks at the school do not speak Spanish, that she can speak enough English to understand much of what they say, and there is sometimes someone in the school to translate. The students are both enrolled in ESL and in a bilingual program, suggesting that the teachers do indeed speak Spanish. Ms. Sanchez relies upon her daughter when she has a problem, she is happy that her children are not involved in gangs or drugs, and that they are learning, though perhaps slowly, in school.

The Sanchez family consists of the parents and 12 children, the oldest of whom is 33 years old and lives in another state. The parents own their home, and rent out two units. During the first visit to the home, Ms. Sanchez asked Jose Luis and Federico whether they had completed their homework, to which Federico replied that he had and Jose Luis that he had not. Jose Luis then went to get his backpack while Ms. Sanchez turned the television on and watched the news in Spanish. While she helped Jose Luis with his work whenever he had a question, the television remained on, making concentration difficult. When Jose Luis completed the work she said "OK," and told him to put his backpack away. Ms. Sanchez seems concerned and willing to help, but perhaps does not realize that the setting and environment are important. She also did not say anything designed to compliment either boy about the schoolwork.

The observers noted that the boys were not at all communicative despite efforts to get them to talk, and that they would not go about their normal business no matter how much the observers assured them that this was fine. One wrote, "Federico was a little bit better at asserting himself, but not much. Jose Luis absolutely could not make a decision." The boys will need to be more confident and self-assured to do well in school, and their parents will need to understand why, and how to help get them there. The boys were hesitant to talk or to show the observers their room or their toys. After some effort though they led the way upstairs to show the toys. It could be that they were nervous and withdrawn because these were strangers, though they had met the observers at Family Focus earlier. I would also note that the boys share a room with their parents (and perhaps a bed), and that their 5-year-old brother was described as very talkative and "rambunctious," unlike his older brothers. The television remained on during the visit, and there was no more discussion of school.

Much of the next visit was devoted to playing games with several other relatives and a few friends before the friends left. Ms. Sanchez was not present during this time, though she was at home when the observer arrived. Mr. Sanchez arrived while the observer asked the boys the questions for the questionnaires and asked him how Jose Luis was doing. Ms. Sanchez later indicated that Federico had a school assignment to complete and asked the observer to help with the assignment, which began with the cutting of a plastic soda bottle to resemble a volcano. When that was complete all of the boys watched the television, though Jose Luis got homework from his backpack and worked on that while watching the television, though the observer noted that he did not seem to be very distracted by the television or by the other boys in the room. Of course, this is not the ideal environment in which to concentrate on schoolwork, and neither Mr. nor Ms. Sanchez paid any attention to Jose Luis during this time. Federico only worked on the volcano, and neither parent worked with him. School was never discussed.

There was no discussion of school during the next visit either, and no schoolwork done. The time was devoted to talking with the boys, watching the television, and drawing pictures. The parents, both of whom were at home, paid little attention to the boys. Much of the next visit was devoted to watching Federico, Jose Luis, and their younger brother play at fighting and wrestling, before going inside to watch the television. No discussion of school, no homework, no chores, no supervised activity.

When the observer arrived for the next visit, music was playing, but the television was not on. Ms. Sanchez asked Jose Luis and Federico to show the observer their report cards, which they did. The cards indicated that neither parent agreed that they read to the students at least 100 minutes a week. We never saw them read to either boy or heard them even discuss school much at all, let alone offer much help with schoolwork. On the other hand, there was not much schoolwork done.

Federico began to work on his homework, while Jose Luis went to a bedroom to watch the television. This is the same Jose Luis who needs to improve in doing his homework. Ms. Sanchez was in the kitchen, and had little interaction with the boys.

Jose Luis and one of his brothers eventually came into the living room to help Federico with his homework for a brief time. Soon Ms. Sanchez left (Mr. Sanchez was outside of the house), and Federico completed the schoolwork and began to watch the television. Later Ms. Sanchez returned and the boys ate dinner as Mr. Sanchez came inside and asked them about their homework. Both Federico and Jose Luis indicated that they had completed their work, though we saw no evidence that Jose Luis had done any homework.

Ms. Sanchez seems concerned with the academic progress of both Jose Luis and Federico, but she does not appear to have a clear notion of just what she should do to help in this process. There is no attention to school or to schoolwork, and no organized activity that might promote responsibility or discipline. Both boys are fairly well behaved, but both quite shy, even withdrawn at times, though this may be more a function of dealing with strangers than anything else. The home environment needs to change to become quieter, more orderly, more attuned to school activity. A parent needs to express consistent interest in every school day, and the homework of the boys. The self-esteem of the boys needs attention consistently, and we saw little evidence of responsibility. There is no effort to emphasize the value of education by either parent, and the boys do not seem to value education very much, but neither do the parents.

For the most part the data collected from the seven families involved in this research suggests a number of issues both in the homes and between the students observed and their parents that have in previous research been associated with poor school performance. Of course, this was not un-expected given that we intentionally selected students doing poorly in school. Jose Rosales is, however, doing fairly well.

As I have indicated above there is a growing body of research that suggests that those concerned with the academic achievement or lack thereof concentrate on the family and its impact on that achievement. As Donna Ford (1993) put it, "future research must place less emphasis on demographic variables at the expense of family values, beliefs, and attitudes." While the families described above are not the same and the efforts to help the parents in them to better prepare their children will therefore not be the same, certain themes have emerged. For the most part, the home environments are not particularly conducive to school-work. Most of the parents do not seem to realize the importance of the self-esteem of their child, or the value of the development of a sense of responsibility or self-control. Few of the parents pay much attention to the schoolwork of the child. Most of the parents indicate that they value the education of their children, but they do not seem to know how to translate that value into behavior and practices that might help the per-formance of the children.

Both Ford (1993) and Dyson (2005) seem to believe that this type of focus on what poor nonwhite families need to do in order to help their children to become more successful academically is a "blame the victim" approach, to use the term used by Ford. Dyson admonished Bill Cosby, the actor, over his "overemphasis on personal responsibility" (p. 69). I clearly do not have the same view. While poverty, race, and ethnicity are still barriers to success, they have not stopped many poor nonwhites from doing well in school. The question upon which I still focus is why some and not others, and the answer almost always comes back to dif-ferences in what goes on or does not go on in the home and with the families. This approach certainly suggests that parents have the primary responsibility for the preparation of their children for school. Obstacles exist for many parents, and these need to be considered when one is try-ing to help parents help children. It is nevertheless my belief based upon the research of many that many families could be helped to help their children do better.

I accept Ford's (1993) position that the family is "a primary socialization agent" (p. 60). In fact, few would argue this position. The family has the main responsibility for preparing the child for the school experience, and I wanted to determine the degree to which families that have apparently not done this well can be helped to do this better. As this chapter shows, not only have most of the families observed here not done this well, but also we have a fairly clear and detailed picture of just what they need to do better.

Part 2

INTERVENTION FOR ACADEMIC SUCCESS

After determining what we believed to be the issues within the home environment and/or the family dynamic that have in past research been associated with poor academic performance, we designed for each family a curriculum that would change the family/home environment in positive ways. That is, we laid out a strategy for each family built around that which we had learned through our initial observations that we believed would help the parents to better prepare their children for the school experience. The curriculum for each family was designed by the staff at the Family Focus centers that had worked with each family in the past, and then reviewed by the author. I felt that it was best to have those professionals who had worked with the families in the past to design the curricula for those families.

Clearly, this strategy would have problems in the real world of academic achievement and the family. It is simply not feasible in any practical sense to design a curriculum for each poor nonwhite family that needs help in learning to better prepare their children for school. This would be very time consuming and expensive. However, in the case of this research it was important to determine whether we could indeed teach parents to better prepare their children. If this is possible, then we can turn our attention to more efficient and less time-consuming strategies, which would no doubt involve meetings with large groups of parents, and more of a cookie-cutter approach. I felt, however, that it was important to first determine whether and to what extent we could make a difference at all. Many well-meaning groups around the country work with parents in an effort to help them to help their children perform better. Much of this work centers on efforts to have the parents more involved in the school activity (Constantino, 2003), but some is focused upon other areas.

According to Henderson and Berla (1994), previous studies of the impact of family involvement in school activities suggests that such involvement has a number of positive outcomes for students. Although this research typically has self-selection issues that cause me to doubt these outcomes in many cases, we are talking about a different type of family involvement altogether. So, while family advocates often try to meet with large numbers of families to encourage and guide them to become involved in their child's educational experience, they have not to my knowledge been in a position to know very specifically what each family needs to do, or to devote the time and staff resources to crafting very specific responses to those needs. While we were able to do that, I still believe that it would not be the most practical or efficient way to approach this for the many families that might need this help. Given that my goal was to determine the degree to which the intervention could make a positive difference, it made sense for research purposes to take this approach.

After a curriculum was devised for each family, again, based upon the initial observations, staff members at the three Family Focus sites decided upon the activities/intervention that were thought to best meet the goals and objectives for each family. Then, they decided upon a timeline for meeting those goals, and just how the success of the intervention would be measured. Originally the intervention phase of the research was to begin in February 2005 and continue until the end of that school year in June 2005. However, near the end of that time period the staff of Family Focus asked to extend the intervention through December, though there was to be little contact with the families during the summer. This would allow the staff 8 months to work with the families. I am certain that school superintendents in large cities who have thousands of poor families who need the kind of intervention and personal attention that we provided would love to have the time and resources to allow 8 months to work with each family. Again, this is not possible in the real world and I am very much aware of this. It was not my goal to provide a blueprint for practitioners, but to determine whether this type of intervention can make a positive difference. I leave the rest to the professionals.

❸

KENDRA ALLEN

As mentioned earlier, Kendra's family has very few of the characteristics associated with high- or average-achieving poor, nonwhite students. Her mother must threaten her in order to have her respond. The house is noisy, unstructured, and chaotic, with minimal discipline and no responsibility. Little schoolwork is done, and Ms. Allen rarely helps with that work. Not only are there no efforts to raise the self-esteem of Kendra, but there seem to be attempts to lower that self-esteem. Kendra does no household chores and has no involvement in extracurricular activities. There was a great deal of work to be done with this family in order to better prepare Kendra for the school experience, and in order for Kendra to perform better in school.

The curriculum for this family reflects the reality that much needed to be done if the family is to learn and to change in order to better prepare Kendra. The goals were as follows: help the family identify a time and a space that would allow Kendra to do her homework and to study after school; help Ms. Allen create a solid base of discipline in the home, and a household structure that encourages and helps Kendra's learning; and support Ms. Allen in her role as a single parent. The discipline, the household structure, and the quiet, orderly place for homework are all characteristics previously identified with academically successful poor nonwhite students (Clark, 1983; Irving, 1990; Ogbu, 2003; Sampson,

2002, 2004), and based upon our initial observations, are all sorely needed in this home.

The support for Ms. Allen in her role as a single parent may well be necessary if she is to be placed in a position to do the other things that research suggests are needed. It is one of the important things I have noted in my earlier work that need to be in place in many poor nonwhite homes if, and perhaps before, the other things that need to change can effectively be altered. A female heads many poor black families, and often when a male is present he plays no positive role in the development of the child. I have noted in my earlier work that it is difficult for a single mother to pay much attention to homework when she must worry about feeding the children, or she is tired from working late to pay the bills. Education professionals often seem to ignore these realities, and assume that every parent is in a position to do the proper things at home if only they knew how and had the required motivation. Unfortunately, it is not that simple.

On the other hand, many families require more than educational professionals can offer. The Allen family needed a lot of help, perhaps more than we could provide if we were to see positive changes in Kendra's performance in the little less than 2 years in which we were involved with the families in this research.

The activities that were identified to meet the various goals of the Allen curriculum were as follows: find an area in the house where Kendra could sit comfortably without the television or radio as distractions; help purchase supplies needed in that area (pens, rulers, calculator); help the family determine what hours Kendra would devote to studying; help the family determine the needed strategies to ensure that the designated area is free of distractions; contact an outside staff person for help and guidance with homework; identify Kendra's disruptive behavior, specify the consequences for this behavior (such as denial of television-watching privileges), and stress that the consequences must be administered consistently; set standards and rules of the household and post those rules and standards; identify specific duties and household chores for which Kendra will be responsible and the consequences for not completing those chores; develop a reward system for positive behavior; hold Kendra responsible for bringing homework home and for turning in completed assignments, with consequences for her failure to comply (such as writing her spelling words 10 times); using exercises from the Self-Concept Workbook to help Kendra improve her self-esteem; develop a weekly calendar of events that relate to the school and the household in order to encourage and enhance the organization of the activities and responsibilities of Ms. Allen; and, finally, to encourage Ms. Allen to participate in scheduled activities, workshops, and parent support groups.

The Family Focus staff members who were designated to implement this ambitious curriculum first met with Ms. Allen in her home in late February of 2005, and there were eight visits made to the Allen home between the end of February and the middle of October of 2005. There were also a number of scheduled visits that were canceled by Ms. Allen, and a number of telephone calls made by the staff to check on progress toward meeting the various goals established in the curriculum and agreed to by Ms. Allen and Kendra during the first home visit by the Family Focus staff.

During the next visit, a staff member noted that Kendra went into the living room, apparently the designated quiet study area, to work on her schoolwork. Instead of getting help with that work from her mother, a staff member provided that help. Previous research has shown that help with homework from the parent is very important because it lets the child know just how important that work and therefore both school and the child are to that parent. Help from the staff member could convey a positive message to the child in terms of self-esteem, but is clearly not the optimum situation. Once I was informed that the staff provided this help, I told them that this needed to stop and that work needed to be done with Ms. Allen to prepare her to provide this help consistently.

The next visit to the Allen home was unannounced because Ms. Allen had cancelled several previous meetings. The staff was concerned that Ms. Allen may have been avoiding them, and therefore avoiding the intervention. Like all of the visits, this visit took place after school. On this day, Ms. Allen played dominos with a relative while Kendra played outside and her siblings played in their rooms. The staff again raised the issue of a quiet study area and they were assured by Ms. Allen that such an area would be provided.

The staff working with Ms. Allen noted on one occasion that Kendra and Ms. Allen had been informed that Kendra might be placed in a learning disabled class because of her behavior. It has been clear that Kendra has behavior problems, and it is not clear at this point that our intervention has helped to ameliorate these problems. It is also true, however, that we have not worked for very long with Kendra and her mother.

During the next visit, a staff member and Kendra worked on her homework, and the staff member advised Kendra to look over that work during the weekend in order to keep it fresh. The staff member noted that Kendra now had a daily planner to help her keep track of her work and designated study/homework times. However, it was noted that a sibling was singing out loud, causing Kendra some distraction. It was also noted that Kendra had an after-school detention for swearing in class. During the next visit, Ms. Allen explained that one of her children was feeling ignored given all of the attention paid to Kendra. The Family Focus staff member suggested that Ms. Allen make certain that she had regular conversations with that child so that she might feel less ignored. Of course, this speaks volumes about the positive attention that seems to be still missing in this household. Indeed, the staff member felt the need to discuss the language used in front of the children by Ms. Allen, and the topics that might not be acceptable conversation topics when children are present. We should perhaps not be surprised that Kendra has been given a detention for using inappropriate language in class when her mother uses inappropriate language in front of her children. This is precisely one of the many things that we needed to change.

The next contact with the family was by telephone, and the staff was informed by Ms. Allen that Kendra was behaving well and that her grades were "consistent." She also informed the staff that since the weather was improving she would be out of the house more often, and therefore the arranged meetings would need to be confirmed beforehand. The staff thought that this was another effort on the part of Ms. Allen to avoid meeting.

During the next meeting, Ms. Allen informed the staff member that she was having serious financial problems, and that Kendra's behavior had improved. I have indicated before that it is often the case that poor parents have difficulty doing the things necessary to help properly prepare their children for school because of the stress of surviving without enough money to pay the light bill or the rent. These parents must devote time, attention, and energy to basic survival issues, leaving less of all three for the children. Still, some manage to do both, and often their children perform well, while others do not. In this case, the staff member made another visit to the Allen home to give Ms. Allen forms that she needed to apply for assistance. In this case the intervention was designed to help Ms. Allen help the family so that she might then be in a better position to devote the required time and energy to helping better prepare Kendra.

During the next visit, the staff member and Kendra sat in the dining room to go over her school project. Asked about her grades, Kendra replied that she had two grades of F. This led to a pep talk from the staff member in which he stressed the importance of doing better in school, and of doing better in everything that she does. It was noted that Kendra had designated a study time, and that she is now completing her homework assignments on time. If both of these observations turn out to be consistent, progress will have been made, albeit a small amount.

The next contact with the Allen family took place in the fall of 2005, because, as I mentioned above, the Family Focus staff asked to continue to work with the families beyond the 2004–2005 academic year, though there was no contact regarding the children during the summer. In retrospect, it might have been a good idea to continue the intervention over the summer, though the direction of such intervention would have been different given that the students were not in school. The concern here is whether any gains made during the academic year were eroded over the summer. This is an issue to be addressed in the future.

When called in the fall of 2005, Ms. Allen asked when the Family Focus staff would return to "help" with Kendra. This does suggest concern on her part for Kendra's progress and welfare. However, when the staff member suggested that Kendra travel to the Family Focus center to work within a group setting, she informed that staff member that transportation was an issue, and that she needed Kendra to help her with the younger children. Again, the realities of poverty have interfered with the school preparation process. Kendra, an 11-year-old fifth-grader is expected to help her mother with younger children, and lacks the transportation to get to a social service center at which staff members want to help her perform better in school. According to the staff member, Ms. Allen was angry that the staff member could no longer help Kendra with her homework, as per my earlier admonitions that we needed to help teach the parents to do this work. It appears that we have yet to accomplish this with Ms. Allen.

When the staff next met with Ms. Allen, she showed them the area of the home that had been designated for Kendra's study, and informed them that this area was the same as it was the past academic year, and that there were to be no distractions. Again, if this continues to be the case, some progress will have been made. The question is whether it has measurable impact on how well Kendra does in school. It is true, however, that it may well be that any positive impact of the intervention may not become apparent until after this research is complete. We have no control over this kind of time frame, and this is one of the problems with the kind of research reported here.

During this visit, however, there was further indication of progress as Ms. Allen noted that while she had allowed the children, including Kendra, to play outside before doing their homework, she recognized that she was wrong to do this. Perhaps she is beginning to understand what she must do if Kendra is to do better in school. On the other hand, when it was time for the children, including Kendra, to come in to do that schoolwork, they were off fighting with another group of children. The staff member and Ms. Allen agreed that it was best if the children did their schoolwork before playing outside, and that Ms. Allen needed to go outside with the children to supervise them. When Ms. Allen told the staff member that Kendra was doing well in school so far though she had no confirmation of this from the school, that staff member suggested that she contact the school to confirm this. This is another of the behavior patterns typically associated with the middle class. They are not just concerned with the education of their children, but are often very comfortable contacting schools to express their concern and to gather necessary information about their children. Many of the poor, however, as Lareau (2003) suggests, fear schools and, I might add, most large institutions. The teachers talk, act, and think quite differently from the manner that many poor folks are accustomed to. This makes many poor parents uncomfortable contacting schools. We are trying to see whether we can teach poor parents to do the same things done by most middle-class parents, and whether and how that will affect the education of their children.

During the final in-home visit, Ms. Allen indicated that she now sits with Kendra every day as Kendra does her homework, and for that received praise from the staff person. Ms. Allen also told the staff member that she did in fact visit the school and was told that Kendra was doing very well. In fact, a number of teachers told her that Kendra was very bright. Of course, being bright is not enough if homework is not completed on time or there are serious behavior problems. Ms. Allen also explained that her children were "full of anger," and as a result she and the children were involved with weekly family counseling sessions. She went on to tell the staff member that Kendra has a bad attitude at home, yet seemed to perform well in school. The staff member explained that Kendra was going through adolescence and probably would benefit from one-on-one time with her mother, and from time to herself with no siblings around. The staff members suggested putting the younger children to bed early and allowing Kendra to remain up for 45 minutes after their bedtime. Ms. Allen said that she would try to accomplish this. The staff member also suggested a way to build communication skills among the family members.

This was in fact the last session with the Allen family, and the question now is the extent to which the intervention was "successful." It is clear that some things appear to have changed/improved based upon the reports of the staff members who worked with the family, and that some appear to have not changed much.

I use the quotation marks with *successful* because I am well aware that there can be honest disagreement about just what success would be in this case, that is, over how to define success. I have defined success as changes in the household dynamic that allow the parent to better prepare her daughter for school, and resulting improvement in the school performance. So, if the intervention were successful in my view, that household would become more like middle-class households, and the child, in this case Kendra, would have better grades, and fewer reported behavior problems. It is also possible that these objectives could be met owing to factors having little to do with the intervention, and that the objectives might not appear to be met within the time frame allotted. Unfortunately, we have no control over these other variables, and had little over the time frame for the research. We were in and out of the homes of these poor families for almost 2 years. While a number of other scholars have observed poor families in their homes over some time, I know of none that have come close to having this number of poor families agree to this kind of interruption for such a long period of time.

These families wanted help; they wanted intervention that might improve the educational experience of their children. However, in this type of research over this time period, there are a number of things that could affect the outcome. A new teacher could motivate the child. A change in the parent's financial condition could have an impact. Still, I contend that if we see positive changes in the household that are related to the goals and objectives laid out for each family, and related to the intervention, then the intervention has had an impact. There may well be lessons here for other poor nonwhite families and for those who want to help narrow the achievement gap between many of them and most white, nonpoor children. Given that we could not use an experimental design, I am comfortable associating changes in the household, improvements in performance, and improvements in behavior to a significant degree to the efforts of the staff members who intervened with the families.

In the case of the Allen family, it appears that the staff accomplished some of the goals put forth in the curriculum developed for the family, and failed to accomplish others. A quiet study area seems to have been set aside for Kendra's use, and Ms. Allen is at least aware of the need both for such an area and for the need for a consistent time period during which Kendra should do her schoolwork. Ms. Allen also seems to be aware of the need for her to work with Kendra on her schoolwork. I have not seen much evidence of the specification of consequences for Kendra's disruptive behavior, the establishment of rules or standards for the household, the identification of household chores that might help develop a sense of responsibility for Kendra, or an improvement in Kendra's self-esteem. It may be that the attention paid to Kendra by the staff will work to improve her self-esteem, but I have not noticed concerted efforts by the staff to accomplish this.

The Allen household is not a middle-class household in the way that I have defined middle-class homes (Sampson, 2004), or in the way that Lareau (2003) has. It was not when we performed the initial observations, and based upon the reports of the interaction by the staff members that worked with the family, it is not one now. On the other hand,

Kendra's grades did improve quite a bit from the time before our attempts to intervene and the time after that intervention. Her final grades at the end of the 2005–2006 academic year were as follows: a D in the Chicago Reading Initiative, a C in writing standards, a C in listening standards, a C in speaking standards, a C in math standards, and Cs in both science and social studies. For the academic year prior to our involvement with the family, all of these grades were Fs and Ds. Now she received grades of A in music and B in physical education. She also showed growth in her habits and her attitudes, according to her grade report. During the third grading period of the 2005–2006 academic year, she needed improvement in five of the nine work habits reported, including following direction and coming to class prepared to work. During the final grading period she needed help in two of these areas, including working in a group and completing assigned classroom work.

Kendra also improved in the social habits reported. During the third grading period, she needed improvement in three of the five habits reported, including exercising self-control, following rules, and accepting teacher guidance. At the end of the year, she needed improvement only in following rules. During the third grading, period Kendra needed improvement in seven of the nine character development areas, including showing care for others, being courteous, and showing respect for herself and others. By the end of the year she needed help only in committing to completing tasks successfully. She still had trouble using conflict-resolution strategies. Whether we measure her improvement by her grades or by her reported behavior, Kendra is doing much better after the intervention than she was before. Is this a function of greater maturity, of a better teacher, of the intervention, of all of these, or of none of these?

The only variable of which we are aware is the intervention. So many things can influence how a child does in school that it is difficult to pinpoint one variable as the only cause of change. However, the society has tried a host of things in an effort to improve the academic success of poor nonwhite students, most of them school based, and for the most part they have failed. Irving (1990) suggests that the "cultural characteristics" of many black students make school success difficult. Comer (1993) writes about the "mainstream culture" as a problem for many. Lareau (2003) refers to "middle-class child rearing" as the key to better performance by the poor and the working class. I have referred to middle-class values, beliefs, and behavior as the key to better performance in public schools, which are, of course, middle-class institutions. It makes sense then to try to help parents who have children performing poorly and whose households and parenting style are not really conducive to higher performance to change those styles and those households. That is what we have done with the Allen household, and though we apparently did not do all that we set out to do, Kendra has performed much better after the help than she did before.

I am inclined to attribute this apparent improvement more to the effects of the almost 2 years of positive attention given to Kendra than to significant changes in either her household dynamic or to changes made by Ms. Allen. For almost 2 years, non–family members came to see her. They let her know that they cared about her, that they believed that she was worth their time, attention, and help. Most poor nonwhite children live everyday in an environment that beats them down, that sends them only negative messages about themselves. Yet, we expect them to overcome this and perform well in an environment that requires relatively high self-esteem, a characteristic hard to come by when your mother pays little attention to you, requires that you care for your infant sibling, and may not know where you are or what you are doing. The Allen household does not seem to be any more middle class as a result of our efforts, but Kendra has done better. Again, I attribute this largely to the long period of positive attention that we gave her.

The second set of observations of Kendra's household did not go as planned. As she so often did, Ms. Allen canceled almost all of the scheduled observations, making it difficult to draw any real conclusions based upon those observations. The observers did note, however, that when they did observe the family, Ms. Allen did most of the talking, rarely allowing Kendra to say much. Ms. Allen led the observers to the dining room, which, by the way, had a nonfunctioning light, so they turned the light in the living room on so that they could see. They noted that the hall leading to the Allen apartment "was filthy and littered with garbage." Their apartment had "a strong smell of urine," and the walls had "noticeable stains and dirt."

The staff member from Family Focus who accompanied the two observers on their first, and as it happens, their only visit to the apartment, showed them Kendra's latest report card and pointed out her improvement. When asked to show her homework, Kendra indicated that she could not find her book bag. The Family Focus staff person told the observers that Kendra really needed attention. This makes sense given that during the almost 2 years that we were in and out of her home, we almost never observed her mother giving her that attention. They were told that she benefited from attention from her father, when she could get that. As is so often the case in poor black households, however, the father is not present in the home. One observer wrote, "[Kendra] is starving for attention." The only positive attention that we could see she received was from our observers and the staff that intervened in her life.

Kendra Allen lives a life that would be difficult for any sixth-grader. Her mother pays little attention to her, rarely engages her in conversation, and expects her to care for her newborn sibling. Her home is often chaotic and dirty, and despite our efforts it is not clear that she has a quiet, orderly place in which to do her schoolwork. There does not seem to be much expected of her. Her mother uses inappropriate language in front of her, and discusses inappropriate topics as well. She then uses inappropriate language in school. According to the second set of observers, Ms. Allen literally bragged that she had confronted Kendra's teachers. Confrontation, while often the response to disagreement from poor folks (Lareau, 2003), does not work well with large institutions such as schools. Kendra does better in school for weeks, according to the Family Focus staff, when she has contact with and attention from her father. Our observations and intervention gave her that kind of positive attention as well. However, ours was research and was not long-term. What will be the source of the needed attention now?

4

IDA SMITH

Ida Smith was a 10-year-old fifth-grader living in the same Chicago neighborhood in which Kendra Allen lived when we first observed her family. As I indicated earlier, she received mainly C and D grades at the end of the 2003–2004 academic year. We observed that her home was structured and orderly, and that her grandmother involved herself in school activities, expected discipline, and not only talked with her children, but encouraged their thoughts. This is something done in most middle-class homes, but not often in non–middle-class homes. Again, many poor children do in fact have this experience, though our society tends to lose sight of this and lump all poor students, particularly poor nonwhite students, together. Based upon our first observations, I believed that the Smith home needed work with self-esteem, providing a quiet place for Ida to study, teaching Ms. Small, her adoptive mother, the value of consistently helping Ida with her homework, and some attention to extracurricular activities.

The curriculum for the Smith–Small family reflected the perception based upon these observations that the family did not need as much as some other families. The major goal of that curriculum was to help the Smith–Small family, led by her grandmother, Ms. Small, to identify an area in the house where Ida can study and complete her schoolwork without interruption from the television or radio. Like a number of the homes of poor nonwhite students who perform poorly in school, the Smith–Small home was not really quiet, and this was a distraction for Ida. The curriculum also indicated that those who were to try to help the family would work with Ms. Smith to help her understand the value of her involvement in reviewing Ida's homework and helping her to prepare for tests. This was all designed to reduce the number of incomplete or missing assignments, to improve Ida's grades, and to help the family help Ida to complete her homework assignments on time.

The first visit in this process took place in late February of 2005, and was basically an introduction to the intervention phase of the research. It was noted that several family members were present, there was a television operating in every room of the house, and there was no designated study area for Ida. Ms. Smith expressed concern that Ida lacked concentration, that she needed to slow down, ask more questions, and complete her assigned schoolwork. While she is concerned, and this concern is quite positive, there was no indication that she turned this concern into action on her part. Ms. Smith did point out that Ida was involved in basketball and in Saturday school, the former an after-school activity that often helps children develop a sense of responsibility and discipline, both needed for success in school. It is clear that Ms. Smith is a parent who has given some thought to what her daughter needs to do in order to perform better in school. This may help her to improve her parenting skills and help Ida improve her educational life.

The next visit took place on the designated date and at the designated time, in contrast to what was often the case in the Allen household. The Family Focus staff person and Ida "immediately" went into the kitchen where Ida began her homework, with help from that staff person, as opposed to help from her grandmother. Actually, the staff person should have been helping Ms. Smith understand the value of her help with that homework. An outside person will not be there everyday over the long haul, and a parent must learn to consistently do those things that better prepare the child for school. Still, a designated study area was set aside for Ida, and there were no family members, loud music, or televisions as distractions for Ida, and the staff person noted, "There was a great deal (of) progress toward keeping the home structured." It appears, then, that Ms. Smith may be learning quickly to do some of the things that she needed to do to help her granddaughter do better in school.

During a subsequent telephone call, Ms. Small indicated that Ida was doing well in school, but that she needed to continue to improve her attitude. During a visit to the home a few days later by one of the staff members, Ms. Small indicated that she needed help to pay several utility bills, and was given information by that staff person that could provide that assistance. All too often, those who write and speak about narrowing the educational performance gap make two serious mistakes: they fail to realize that many poor nonwhite students are doing fine as they lump all of them together, and they fail to take into consideration the impact that poverty has on families on an everyday basis. We are asking families like the Smith–Small family to somehow ignore the reality that they may not be able to pay a gas or electric bill and concentrate on helping Ida with her homework, perhaps in an unlighted, cold house. In the case of this research, we are trying to determine the effectiveness of efforts to teach poor parents to act like middle-class parents when poverty makes this difficult for them. On the other hand, Ms. Small told the staff person that Ida was doing better in school, and that staff person told Ms. Small that this improvement was to a significant degree due to her efforts.

During the next home visit, Ida and the staff member worked on her reading in the kitchen, and then Ida completed her other homework assignments while the staff member watched. She was then shown her mistakes and corrected them herself. Her school progress report that was shown to the staff member indicated improved performance. Ida also mentioned that her birthday was soon, and she was happy that she would spend the day with her father. Kendra Allen was also very happy to visit with her father, but all too often in the poor black homes that I have studied, the father is not a significant factor. This places an enormous burden upon the mother, who must be all things for all of the children, and makes "middleclassness" that much more difficult to achieve.

During the next visit to the home by the staff person assigned to help support the family, Ms. Small again indicated that Ida's grades had "greatly" improved, as had her self-esteem. As was the case for Kendra Allen, months of attention by non–family members whose stated goal is to teach the family how to help Ida do better appears to raise the self-esteem of the child, and this helps improve school performance. The question of course is whether these changes will last after that intervention is complete. I suspect that they can if the parent begins to play the role of the person who intervenes, but that parent must be taught to do this. It is possible that these lessons can be learned, by example, with the parent learning by watching and listening to the staff person, assuming that the parent is interested in learning.

During this visit the staff person and Ms. Small discussed material dealing with adolescent development, so she was not just learning by example. She was also being directly taught to do some of the things that she needed to do in order to help Ida do better in school. Ms. Small again indicated that she had financial problems, and the staff person told her that she was aware of a program that might offer assistance. The next visit with Ida took place at her school, where she was involved with the Sister-To-Sister Program, a national program that attempts to "try new things outside of the classroom" that may help young women by building supportive relationships. So, Ida apparently has other forms of support as well as that from her mother and Family Focus. After the study time for the students involved with Sister-To-Sister was finished, the participants went outside to play.

During the next visit to Ida's home she and the staff person went over her math work, and discussed her report card, both things that Ms. Small should have been urged to do, and would need to be taught to do for the future. The staff person did note that Ida's report card "was very impressive." There were no checks indicating poor behavior, and some of her grades had improved by two letter grades. Positive and consistent attention indicating concern for her clearly has made a difference in her school performance.

The next visit to the Smith–Small household took place in the fall of 2005, after the summer vacation. When Ida arrived home, she went directly to the designated study area. After she put her book bag down though, she proceeded to the kitchen for a snack. After eating she asked Ms. Small who was going to help her with her homework. This is a very positive sign because it suggests that Ida now expects help with her work, perhaps from her grandmother, and that her grandmother is sufficiently involved with Ida's education to be asked about this. In fact, it was Ms. Small who helped with the work. It appears that a corner has been turned in this home. Ida has a designated study area, she knows that she is expected to use this area for study when she arrives from school, and she now expects her grandmother to go over that work with her.

All of this is characteristic of higher-achieving poor nonwhite homes. Ms. Small did indicate that Ida has mood swings, and was told by the staff person that this is common for young girls going through puberty, and suggested that her menstrual cycle may begin soon if it had not already. When the staff person suggested individual counseling for Ida, Ms. Small stated that if Ida's mood swings did not change she would consider the counseling. Ms. Small is not only concerned and attentive, but seems willing to translate that concern into action that may help Ida perform better.

Ms. Small indicated during the next session, at which Ida was not present, that Ida was involved in several after-school activities, and therefore not at home. Those activities include the Big Sister program. She also told the staff person that Ida now has a regular routine that centers around going straight to her study area to work on her schoolwork when she does not have after-school activities. She also noted that either she or her daughter sits with Ida each day to help with that work, and that her grades and reported attitude are both improving, though some teachers said that she still needed some work with her attitude. Ms. Small informed the staff person that Ida's cycle had in fact begun the previous month, and that she now pays greater attention to the mood swings. This is progress. Ms. Small has learned valuable lessons about puberty that may well help her help Ida do better. The staff person suggested that Ms. Small talk with Ida about the changes that she is confronting. This is the kind of discussion between parent and child that is common in middle-class homes, but as Lareau (2003) points out, is not often observed in poor households. It is also the kind of interaction that helps children to do better in school, in part because it sharpens critical thinking skills and in part because it helps with the use of language.

Ms. Smith was encouraged to enroll Ida in a pregnancy prevention program, and to herself attend a grandparents-raising-children program, and she agreed to do both, indicating that she needed all of the support available. This seems to be a woman who wants to learn and to do those things that will help her help Ida perform better and, by all accounts, has learned some of those things.

The final two sessions took place at Ida's school and did not involve her grandmother, so no real training of Ms. Small could take place. Ida was involved again in the Sister-To-Sister program after school, as well as the Male Responsibility Program. After she went over her homework with the help of the Family Focus staff person assigned to her family, she led the group discussion by asking questions and even challenging her peers to participate. This suggests not only a fairly high level of confidence/self-esteem, but perhaps leadership ability as well, characteristics that will serve her well in school and in life.

However, during the next session at school, Ida appeared "grumpy" and told the staff person that her teacher got "on her nerves" because she handed out too much homework. When asked to talk with the staff member about that work, she told him that she had no real problem with the work, but that she simply did not want to do the work, she would prefer to eat her candy. The staff member went over the ground rules for the intervention, and Ida agreed to wait to eat the candy until the session was complete, showing some discipline and ability to delay gratification.

At the beginning of the 2005–2006 academic year, near the end of our intervention efforts, Ida received a C in the Chicago Reading Framework, compared to a D at the end of the 2003–2004 year. She received a B+ in writing standards, Cs in listening, speaking, and math, a C− in science, and a D+ in social science. At the end of the 2005–2006 academic year, when our intervention efforts were complete, she had a D in the Reading Initiative, a C− in writing, a C in listening, a D in research standards, a C+ in math, a C in science, and an F in social science. However, she received a B− in conduct and a C for her homework.

The only improvement that Ida needed in her habits and attitudes was in accepting teacher guidance. In the fall of the 2005–2006 year, she needed to improve in 14 of the 23 habit and attitude categories. It seems to be the case that Ida's behavior has improved in school, but her grades are spotty. There was improvement, then regression. It is therefore difficult to conclude that the intervention helped in terms of performance, at least not short-term. However, the improvement in her attitudes and behavior offer hope for improvement in the longer term.

Too often, poor nonwhite students are seen by teachers and administrators as behavior problems, and are consequently not taught well because it is thought that that effort will be a waste of time and energy. They very often do not behave the way middle-class students tend to behave, in part because they are not raised the same way, and in part because they face obstacles not faced by most middle class–middle income children who do not have to contend with not enough money to pay rent or utility bills or with the absence of a father. As we have noted in the past (Sampson, 2002, 2004), this is not the case for all poor nonwhite students, and I cannot write this often enough. Still, it is the reality for most of them, but it does not appear that this is true in the case of Ida Smith. Her behavior is no longer a problem for her or for her teachers, though we see little significant change in her grades as yet. Have things changed in her home in ways that might benefit her in school as a result of the intervention?

Unlike the situation with the Allen family, we were able to observe the Smith–Small family several times in February 2006 and March 2006. During the first visit of the second set of observations, the observer noted that Jake, a young boy who seemed to be about 4 or 5 years old, played with a friend from upstairs who was a little older, but Ida was not at home. She apparently had gone to visit her mother. Two television sets were on in the apartment, and there were bunk beds in the living room. Ms. Small's husband and a teenaged boy were also in the apartment. The two young boys were very interested in the observer, a black male, asking him several questions, including whether he was a pimp.

At one point Jake, the 4- or 5-year-old was told by Mr. Small to stop doing something, but Jake told him that he would not stop. The observer was struck by the apparent lack of discipline. While the young boys played and the two adults watched the televisions, the teenaged boy was preparing dinner. Ms. Small told the observer that Ida now went to a hospital throughout the week, and that she was, as a result, not attending school. She had been suspended from school a number of times due to her behavior, and the school staff had recommended that Ida receive an evaluation from the hospital, where the staff had recommended that Ida be brought during the week so that she could be observed.

All of Ida's schoolwork was being completed at the hospital, which apparently provided her education now. Ida is taken to the hospital Monday through Thursday in the morning, and returns in the early evening. Ms. Small is somewhat leery of the hospital because she does not want Ida medicated if that medication "messes up the mind." Apparently, what seemed to be improvements in Ida's school behavior and attitude have not lasted.

Ida was at home during the next visit, and Ms. Smith informed the observer that she was now back at school with a great deal of homework to complete. When asked about that homework by Ms. Small, Ida replied that she did in fact have science homework to do, but rather than doing that work, Ida played a video game, despite the urging of her grandmother to start the work. She also refused to answer the telephone when told to do so by Ms. Small. After some time watching the television, Ida was again told by Ms. Small to do her schoolwork, and this time she complied, though she did so while sitting in front of the television, which was still on, and stopped that work after a few minutes to continue watching the television.

Ms. Smith told the observer that she thought that Ida may need counseling as a result of her continuing behavior problems, which she thought were caused at least in part by others exerting negative influence on Ida. If Ida did not change her behavior soon, according to Ms. Small, she might have to consider a permanent stay at the hospital. This was discussed while Ida sat and listened. When Ida was interviewed a year and a half earlier by the first observer, she did mention that other students at school had tried to prevent her from doing well, and had pressured her to skip school. It may well be that Ida has given in to peer pressure to avoid doing well in school, but we have no way to really confirm this. We do know that she shows little discipline at home and that she has serious behavior problems at school.

When Ms. Small asked Ida about her school day, she initially did not answer, then when asked a second time said that she had done math, reading, and science. There was no more discussion of school, though Ida did return to her science work a bit later, while still watching the television. Ida asked her grandmother whether she would attend her basketball game the next day and was told that she would not. The observer noted that Ida seemed very proud of her basketball uniform that was in her book bag. Ms. Smith, however, paid little attention to this fact, and missed an opportunity to help boost Ida's self-esteem, something sorely needed.

At one point Ida watched the television, listened to the radio, and talked on the telephone while Jake ran around the apartment playing. Clearly, the apartment was not the quiet, orderly, structured environment conducive to serious schoolwork. Although Ms. Smith told the observer that she believed that children today lack discipline, she showed little inclination to discipline either Ida, Jake, or his friend. However, according to the observer, she did threaten them on occasion, in particular Jake because of his "constant" temper tantrums. She also told Ida that if her behavior did not improve she might have to stay at the hospital permanently. This kind of threatening behavior is not common among the middle class, whether they are poor or middle-income. Middle-class parents are more likely to discuss with and explain to children. Of course, middle-income parents are more likely than others to have the time, verbal skills, and lack of pressure that allow them to discuss rather than to direct or to yell, as Mr. Small did on occasion.

If, however, we want poor children to perform well in middle-class institutions such as public schools, they will need to be able to discuss, to think critically, to question, to feel confident enough to explore, and to question. This requires a home environment conducive to the development of these characteristics, an environment very much unlike what we now see in Ida's apartment, despite the good intentions of her grandmother. The discipline is not there. The structure is not there. There is no discussion, and little regulation of impulses. There is little delayed gratification, little tolerance for frustration. These are all, as Comer (1993) refers to them, "lines and pathways" of development that "facilitate academic learning and preparation for life" (p. 304). These are middle-class characteristics, though some black scholars see them as white characteristics, and see the notion that some poor blacks could benefit from taking on some of the characteristics of middle-class families as a form of class warfare (Dyson, 2005).

I do not believe that whites have a corner on the market of middle-class attitudes, beliefs, or behavior, and if they do then we should stop the discussion of narrowing the performance gap between (some) poor nonwhites and many middle-income whites. As long as public schools remain middle-class institutions, or "instruments of the mainstream culture" (Comer, 1993, 305), those who have mastered the values and ways of that culture will do better than most others. Lareau (2003) makes it clear that middle-class children are better at this than others owing to the child-rearing patterns of their parents, and many poor black and poor Latino parents raise their children this way, making the middle-class-as-white argument not only spurious, but a bit dangerous as well given that we want poor nonwhite children to succeed. While scholars such as Dyson (2005) write naively, but politically correctly, about "black culture" as though there is actually one such culture, many little black children are failing.

As I have indicated earlier in this work, the realities of poverty often push school success to the background for many poor families. The reality of waking up every morning worrying about the utilities being turned off, or where food will come from, or knowing that no other person believes that you are worthwhile gets in the way of academic success for many, and these realities must be confronted. Still, it does not get in the way for all, and society needs to learn from those who manage to overcome the realities, and use these lessons, as we attempt to do here, to help others to do so as well.

During the next visit, Mr. Small sat at his normal place in front of a television, and as Jake asked repeatedly to change the channel he was ignored. When Jake tried to do so while Mr. Small was not paying attention, Mr. Small promptly scolded him, though Mr. Small, who was called by his first name by all of the children in the apartment, eventually capitulated for a short time. Ida arrived after a time, accompanied by the young neighbor, and began her homework on one of the bunk beds in the living room near the television that was dark. When her teenaged brother arrived with Ms. Small, he scolded Ida for working on her schoolwork in the dark and turned on the light. Her grandmother did ask about her schoolwork and Ida replied that she was doing it at that time. After some 20 minutes, her older brother Allen along with Ms. Small checked her homework. It appears that Ms. Small is concerned with how Ida is doing in school, and that she occasionally checks that work and works with her, but this activity needs to be consistent, and the intervention has apparently not accomplished this.

Allen "was somewhat hard" on Ida for her mistakes, according to the observer, and though he offered to help her correct the mistakes, she told him that she did not need his help. When Ms. Small told Ida that she had mistakes in her reading homework, she and Ida argued about this, with Ida, apparently jokingly, telling Ms. Smith that they would fight about this when the observer left, and that she had been looking for a fight all day. She did not correct the mistakes pointed out by Ms. Small and corrected only one of those on her math work pointed out by Allen.

Ida told Allen several times that evening that her basketball team was undefeated, a fact that made her clearly proud, but no one discussed this with her, no one congratulated or encouraged her or tied her participation to the quality of her schoolwork. Later Ida turned the radio on while they all watched the television, and attempted to use the telephone. The noise and distractions seem to be a constant, as they were during the next visit as well. Ms. Small did ask Ida whether she had homework, and when Ida told her she did not, Ms. Small asked her why, but she did not answer her.

Ms. Small then asked Ida to read to Jake, something that we noticed she did when we first observed the family in the fall of 2004. While Ida read to Jake, they both watched the television, and changed the channel often despite admonitions from his grandmother to not change the channel. "It seems from my observations that (Jake) does whatever he really wants to do," wrote the observer. The discipline that we have seen in the homes of poor Latino and poor black families in which the students do well in school is not consistently present here. After reading and watching the television, Ida read her own science book for a few minutes while continuing to watch the television.

Later Ms. Small curses as she refers to a television show, only to have Jake curse as well. While Allen and Ms. Small both tell him not to curse, he does so again. He also has a temper tantrum when Allen refuses to give him his way, but calms down when Ms. Small directs Allen to allow him to have what he wants. Not only are the efforts at discipline only half-hearted, but it appears that neither Ida nor Jake have learned to delay gratification or to tolerate frustration well. There is no discussion between the adults and the children that would help them learn to think critically, or to question, or to feel confident about their speaking and thinking ability when dealing with non–family members.

The Small home is always neat and clean, unlike the Allen home, but there is always the noise from the television as well, noted the observer about the next and final visit to the home. When Jake throws his shoes on the floor he is promptly told by Ms. Small to pick them up. Again, she does require some discipline, but it seems that she is inconsistent and does it without explanation. Ida again begins her homework without prodding, but the television is on as she does this work, as is the radio for some of the time.

While Ida watched, listened, and did her homework, Ms. Small talked on the telephone about the No Child Left Behind Act and educational funding, clear indication of not only her interest in education but some knowledge as well. While all of this was happening Ida completed her schoolwork and asked the observer whether he wanted to look at that work. When the observer declined, she asked Ms. Small whether she wanted to examine the work, only to have her ask the observer to check it. One of the major goals of the intervention was to help Ms. Small to understand the value of and need to have her work with Ida on her schoolwork. This has not happened. Another goal was to identify a place in the home where Ida could do her homework without interruption from the television or radio. This has not happened either. We wanted to teach the family the value of deciding what hours everyday Ida would devote to schoolwork, and Ida does her homework, when she does any, at about the same time daily.

It is noteworthy that during this visit, Ms. Small talked with a visitor about recent shootings in a different Chicago neighborhood. It is easy to suggest that poor families find a quiet place for study, but the reality is that when the living room is also the bedroom for some, finding that place is not that easy. It is easy to suggest that parents concentrate on helping to teach children delay gratification, but in the real world of murders of young girls and pimps, this may not be so easy to accomplish. While I have found that some families manage to do these things despite the obstacles, these obstacles must be considered.

During this visit, Jake's friend was yelled at several times by Ms. Smith, while Jake was threatened with a belt for his behavior, which, by the way, he continued despite the threats. In 2004 when we made the first observations of the Small home I noted that Ida consistently did her homework as well as read to Jake. The home was orderly and structured, though not quiet. Ida was expected to think, Ms. Small expected discipline from Jake, and she was aware of current events. The second observations provided little to change this view, though there are questions about the consistency of the discipline. Ida seems to have continuing behavior problems at school though her report card suggests that these are under control. It is not really clear that the intervention accomplished the things that we wanted to accomplish with this family. It is, of course, difficult to determine whether this is a function of the intervention or the family or both.

Ida appears to be thoughtful and resourceful, Ms. Small is concerned, but often not really helpful to Ida or to Jake for that matter. The kind of "concerted cultivation" that Lareau (2003) writes is characteristic of middle-class homes and typically leads to better academic performance is not present here, and our intervention apparently has not helped develop it, at least not in the short term. Ms. Small does not nurture the development of the social and cognitive skills prized in schools despite our efforts. Again, when the discussion is about the murder of two young girls as well as No Child Left Behind, or the concern is about money to pay the utilities or whether an observer is a pimp, the reality of poverty seems to get in the way for many.

I did not observe either Ms. Allen or Ms. Small interacting with the school system, though Ms. Allen was proud that she had confronted Kendra's teachers, but confrontation does not work well in large, complex institutions. Ida receives positive attention from her older brother and from her grandmother, but there is little effort to develop the ability to delay gratification, or to systematically boost her self-esteem, from her grandparents, even when easy opportunities to do so present themselves. Growing up poor and black in America is exceptionally difficult for most poor black children, given the constant struggles to survive that often accompany poverty, and the feelings of worthlessness and/or doubt that often accompany being black. High self-esteem is critical for all students, but particularly for poor black and, to some degree, for poor Latino students. Ida is proud of herself as a result of her basketball accomplishments, but Ms. Small seems to pay these accomplishments little attention, when she could use them to work on the self-esteem of Ida. We have apparently not been very successful in helping her to understand this lesson, or the others that we wanted to "teach." The same concerns that we had in 2004 are there 2 years later, as are the same strengths in the home environment. The report card and Ms. Small suggest that Ida is doing better in terms of her attitudes and behavior during and after the intervention, but the fact that Ida has had to visit the hospital for evaluation apparently as a result of that behavior, and that she had been suspended a number of times from school, raises questions about this improvement.

We did not see any behavior on her part that would suggest serious problems. She was not always obedient, and she occasionally was somewhat sneaky, but she is not a quiet, retiring child who desperately needs attention. Clearly, more work is needed here.

5

JASON GREEN

Jason was a 9-year-old fourth-grader in Evanston when we first observed him, and he was below grade level in almost half of the reading,
math, writing, and science categories, though he had no real behavioral
problems. The curriculum for his family focused on finding a quiet,
well-lit space at his home at which he can do his homework, making certain that he does his schoolwork in 30-minute intervals, referring him to
the 21st Century Program, referring the family to a Family Resource
Coalition, and supporting his mother in dealing with the Individualized
Education Program (IEP) staff. The 21st Century Program is a commu-
nity-based program designed to provide academic enrichment chances
for children in poor neighborhoods or attending underperforming
schools, while the IEP is a program for students who either have dis-
abilities or who receive special education or related services. It was
thought that Jason had trouble concentrating on his schoolwork for long
periods of time, and that teaching him and his mother to divide the work
into 30-minute intervals might help with his concentration. Like most of
the poor children involved in this research, Jason's home environment is
often full of distractions, making it difficult for the student to concentrate, and it was believed that the identification of a particular place
without these distractions would also help him.

The intervention by the Family Focus staff person began in late February of 2005, with Jason's mother absent. Jason was being cared for this time by his grandmother, who asked him right away about his day at school, and whether he had completed his homework. She informed the staff person that while she may not always be able to help Jason, she always wanted to know whether he had homework and whether he had completed the work. As I have indicated a number of times, this attention is important both for the self-esteem of the child and in letting the student know how important education is. The staff person noted that Jason is very shy, had low self-esteem, and was not comfortable asking her for help with his work. She, therefore, asked him to read to her, but this was difficult because according to her Jason could not read very well at all. Remember, Jason was in the fourth grade. In our initial observations, we realized that Jason was very shy, but we did not believe that his self-esteem was low.

Jason found a number of things other than homework to do, preferring to talk about art or to draw and to watch the television, which he was not allowed by his grandmother to do until he had completed the schoolwork. It would have been difficult to work with his mother to identify the homework space given that it was not really clear who had the primary child-rearing responsibilities. In fact, it would have been somewhat difficult to carry out most of the intervention activities.

By the time the staff person next visited the Green family, they had moved to a different, larger apartment. When she arrived at the apartment neither his mother nor grandmother were home from work, and a babysitter was in charge of the children. So, the staff person was now working with a new space and a non–family member, though the babysitter and the staff person "cleaned a space for him to do his homework." Of course, it would have been preferable for the mother to do this so that this space might be permanent. Jason and the babysitter struggled with his homework for some time, before the staff person helped. She then gave him several books to read with his mother for 15–20 minutes every night. This was designed to help with his reading skills, and to promote the kind of caring and nurturing relationship that most middle-class parents have with their children. Such attention helps children to become more confident and to understand just how much the parents care about them. After she left the apartment, the staff person encountered Ms.

Green and informed her that it was very important that she was at home to work with Jason. She agreed to be there during the next visit, but she would not be available for over a month.

There seemed to be very little mothering here, and little opportunity to help Ms. Green to understand the things that she needed to do if she wants to help Jason do better in school. She has indicated that school is important, but is not available to learn to translate that belief into action. The next time that the observer saw Ms. Green was at a 21st Century family night that Jason attended with her. The staff person noted that Ms. Green preferred to sit and talk with her friends rather than to sit with Jason, even though she had been informed by the staff person that it was important for her to spend time alone with Jason, to ask about his day, about his schoolwork, to show some interest in and concern for him.

Jason had very low writing skills, was a loner, and was often very quiet, according to the staff person, who purchased a handwriting workbook for him to work with over the summer. The staff person offered this type of financial assistance, but Ms. Green should have understood the importance of the reading and how much help her son needed. She apparently did not, and showed little interest in learning to do so. Ms. Green was looking for work, and given that she had moved to a different apartment felt that she had to find a job soon or risk losing the apartment. She also had a baby and devoted most of her attention to the baby, and very little to Jason. Indeed, the staff person observed that Jason might not perform better in school because he was trying to get the attention of his mother in any way that he could, including poor school performance. If this was his goal, it did not work! While he seemed to want her to ask about his day, to sit with him while he did his schoolwork, to spend time alone with him, and while we had told her several times how important these things were and why, she did not do them.

Jason was enrolled in the 21st Century Summer Reading Intensive Program with the help of the staff person, who also gave him a tape recorder so that he can hear himself read. Ms. Green was told again that she must give him uninterrupted time everyday, even during the summer break, during which the staff person has asked him to work on reading and writing. The reality of poverty surfaced early in the fall for the Green family as the observer noted that Ms. Green had begun to drink heavily again, and was without a job, again. At a public event she had to be restrained, much to Jason's embarrassment, and someone else took Jason home. While his pride was clearly hurt, the staff person indicated that he has grown in the past year or so, but also noted that Ms. Green needed outside help. His grandmother assured her that she would make certain that Jason would devote 20 minutes a day to his homework, without distractions, given that he had "slacked off" from the agreed-upon 30 minutes.

In the fall of the 2005–2006 academic year, his fifth-grade teacher indicated that Jason was having "a stellar year in many areas." He was at grade level in six of the seven reading categories, four of the five writing categories, all of the three listening and speaking categories, nine of the eleven math categories, all of the three science categories, and all of the four social science categories. Jason's behavior was satisfactory in all but two of the nine behavior and work habit categories, needing improvement in working independently and completing his homework on time. Overall, it appears that Jason is now an average student, and his teachers' comments on his grade report for the 2005–2006 academic year indicates that he is capable of doing even better. The teacher wrote, "His comprehension and fluency have improved and his attitude toward school is outstanding." He also wrote, "His average word score is 64% even though he is capable of 90–100%." The comments make several references to the negative impact on Jason's attitude and performance of recent events, "home and friendship issues," and the need to build support at home.

Based then upon the school progress report Jason is doing better in school now than he did before the intervention, and his behavior was never a real problem. While I shall need to return to this issue again I need to point out that Kendra Allen received very little positive attention from her mother and had serious behavior problems, while Jason received very little positive attention from his mother and had few behavior problems. Ida Smith performed better after she received positive attention from adults. Clearly, attention and the impact that it has on self-esteem for the children are very important, but the relationship is obviously quite complicated. All three of the children observed thus far needed more attention, but one of them had few problems in school without the attention, while two struggled mightily.

It is also becoming obvious that the role of our intervention is not nearly as clear as I thought it might be. We have not been able to teach these three families to value, believe, and behave in the ways that help most middle-class children perform well in school. So far, I would have to say that we cannot simply turn these families into middle-class families with children doing well in school by trying to teach them the value of self-esteem or delayed gratification, or helping the student with homework, responsibility, discipline, or involvement with extracurricular activities. On the other hand, it may well be that these families observed so far simply have not wanted badly enough to learn, and/or that they have not been in a position to learn given their serious other problems, many related to their poverty. While it is possible that the impact of the intervention could show up later, I rather doubt that possibility.

I am not certain that the intervention has been all that it could have been either. The focus upon creation of a quiet, orderly space in the homes for the homework of the child makes sense, and it appears that the emphasis upon having Jason do his school work in 30-minute intervals has paid off, but I believe we missed opportunities to stress to the parents or guardians the value of taking advantage of opportunities to boost the self-esteem of the students, or to teach them the value of frustration avoidance or delayed gratification. We saw a number of these opportunities in the apartments, but said little or nothing when we did. It would have been difficult, however, to do this consistently when Jason's mother was seldom present or Kendra's mother was simply not paying attention.

These three families have financial and emotional issues that have made school success a lesser priority, though the parents and grandparent have signaled their concern for that success by allowing us in their homes for almost 2 years, off and on. These issues need to be addressed if the families are to have the time, energy, and commitment required to make the needed changes. We see some progress during and after the intervention, but in two of the cases we also see some troubling things. Did the intervention have any impact upon the home environment of Jason?

We began the observations designed to provide an answer to that question in early February of 2006 with the new observer meeting with Jason, Ms. Green, and two younger siblings at their grandmother's home, with whom they were apparently living at the time. When Ms. Green asked Jason whether he had any homework, Jason began to work on his reading material. Soon after, Ms. Green turned on the television and began dancing to the music of the videos with the two younger children. Jason alternately worked on his reading, watched the television, and discussed with his mother who sang a particular song. He then returned to reading, while Ms. Green told the observer how much he liked to read. They also discussed upcoming school events, and Jason mentioned his basketball practice, suggesting that he is involved in extracurricular activities.

A bit later, Jason talked with the observer about his book club and worked for a few minutes on his math, but the observer noted that he never worked on anything for more than 10 or 15 minutes, something that his teacher had suggested was a problem. His teacher also indicated that Jason had a tendency to "give up on himself," and that he needed support at home. We did not see this support, nor was the quiet, structured area to do his homework in place.

When the observer arrived for the next visit several weeks later, Jason was again watching a television game show. When Jason knew the answer to one of the questions, Ms. Green congratulated him. He then told his mother about his day, including the fact that a friend's father had taken the two of them to a local museum. It is interesting that Ms. Green did not appear to know what her son had done that day even though there was no school. While she filled out some forms, she did stop to ask Jason whether he had any homework, but he indicated that he had completed the work at the 21st Century session. He and the observer then played a board game while the two younger children constantly interrupted them. Ms. Green told them to stop, but they ignored her. It may well be that Ms. Green has learned from the intervention to consistently ask Jason about his day.

While this helps to show Jason that his mother is interested in him and his work, the fact that Ms. Green does not help with the homework, or seem to know much about what Jason is doing, is problematic and was not successfully addressed by the intervention. During the next visit, Jason worked on a craft in which he is interested; he also read and watched the television, before beginning to play a game. The observer noted, as had the staff person from Family Focus, that Ms. Green pays much more attention to the younger siblings than to Jason. All indications are that Jason needs the kind of attention from his mother that Kendra needs from hers, and that Ida needs from her father, but none of them receive the attention consistently.

It might be possible for each of them to receive this needed attention from another adult, a volunteer, or a person from a social service agency. They, however, would not be with the student consistently and probably not for the long term. It is something to be considered if the parents and grandparent will not or cannot provide this support and attention.

The next meeting began at Jason's school because he had a parent–teacher conference that day, and the observer sat in on the conference. His teacher indicated that Jason had been doing very well at the start of the school year, but had "fallen in with some troublemakers," and was influenced by children who did not think that school was important. In response, Ms. Green suggested that the teacher use some form of corporal punishment, to which the teacher responded that that was not a good idea. Rather than seriously discuss the problem with the teacher or Jason, Ms. Green not only resorted to the "solution" often preferred by non–middle-class parents—beating—but she also suggested that the teacher do this.

Of course, punishment is not the teacher's responsibility, but hers, and it is probable that punishment is not the solution to the problem. This is the second time that we have had some indication of peer pressure on one of the students observed to perform poorly in school. While much has been written and said about the impact of this pressure, particularly on poor black children, I have not seen a great deal of evidence of this in my research. The argument is that there is a culture of failure among poor blacks, who may not see educational success as particularly valuable given that they actually see or know very few blacks for whom it has done much good. They can use as an excuse for failure that "the system" or the teachers are biased against blacks. This excuse only works as long as most blacks perform poorly. Thus, the idea that there is pressure to perform poorly on many of those who can and sometimes do perform well.

When a student lives in an area in which it is the pimps and the drug dealers that are "successful," there may be little incentive to view education as important. Still, many poor nonwhite students do see the value of education and, if the right things are in place at home, manage to perform well. It seems that Jason has the ability. His teacher told Ms. Green that Jason was college bound. Notice, it seems to be the teacher with the confidence in Jason, the teacher who works to boost his self-esteem, not Ms. Green, despite our efforts to teach her to do so. The teacher discussed with Ms. Green a fifth-grade camp, and offered to make some arrangements for the costs of the camp. Ms. Green did ask about Jason's relationship with one of his friends, and was told that the two of them are sometimes in trouble together, to which Ms. Green replied to Jason that he needed to concentrate on school during school hours, and leave the play with the friend for after-school hours. Jason promised to ignore those students that might adversely affect his performance, and to work harder in the next term.

When they returned home, Jason wanted to make certain that he had the permission slip for a field trip signed, and that he had transportation to an upcoming basketball game. There are strong indications that he is a disciplined, thoughtful, responsible young man but that his mother is struggling with her role. Before the observer left, Ms. Green told him about a serious financial problem that she had. Poor parents often have more serious and more important things to attend to than helping a student with homework, or working on her self-esteem. The time and the energy for these things are often luxuries for many poor families. Yet, they must be done if the students are to do well in school.

During the final visit, Ms. Green asked Jason how he had done on a practice state-mandated standardized test, to which he replied that he had done fine. There was no more discussion of the test, no talk about the significance of the test. Jason showed his mother his word test, for which he had received a grade of 39 out of a possible 42, and for which he was visibly proud. This time Ms. Green indicated that she too was proud, but instead of using the opportunity to discuss with Jason his talents, his skill, his accomplishments, she asked him to show the test to the observer. It seems that she could have made better use of this little opportunity to work on Jason's self-esteem, exactly the kind of lesson that the intervention was designed to teach, but very often did not. Ms. Green did review Jason's day, but then everyone turned to the television.

During our initial observations of the Green family, we found that their home was often noisy and very busy, and the current home is the same. The observer noted that Ms. Green shows much more affection for and gives more attention to the younger siblings than to Jason, and that has not changed. Ms. Green pointed out to that observer that her son loves to read, and she did the same with the second observer. Jason was thoughtful and helpful then, and he is now. Apparently, not much has changed about the home environment as a result of the intervention. Ms. Green thinks quite highly of Jason, but misses many opportunities to let him know that. This has not changed. She still does not help with his homework, though she still asks about that work fairly consistently. She does not challenge him to think or discuss much with him. She pays almost no attention to his extracurricular activities or to his interests. There were some positives in place when we began the work with this family, and they are still in place. However, the negatives have apparently not been really overcome. Where school is concerned, the family still behaves as most poor families behave, and not as most middle-class families behave.

On the other hand, Jason is doing better in school, though I would not attribute this to changes at home. He is involved with several programs designed to offer him help, and perhaps it is these programs coupled with the attention from the Family Focus staff person and the observers that have helped him. It was our goal to determine the extent to which efforts to help the family behave more like middle-class families where education is concerned could be successful. If they were, I expected that the students would perform better in school. So far, the results are not clear.

6

ANITA TERRY

When we began this research, Anita Terry was a 10-year-old fifth-grader in Evanston who thought that math was boring, disliked boys because they called her ugly, and expected to go to college even though her grades were very poor. She indicated that she devoted about 20 minutes a day to homework, lives with her maternal grandmother (Ms. Robbins) who is her legal guardian, and was not observed to care much about school. She has little structure at home, self-esteem issues, little discipline, and had recently experienced a family tragedy that deeply affected her.

As was the case for each family studied thus far, the curriculum for the family began with the goal of helping the family identify a time and a place for Anita to study and to do homework after school. The space was to be without disruption. The curriculum also included assisting the family in deciding the hours that Anita would devote to study, helping Anita develop an academic journal that would keep track of her assignments and their completion, and helping the family enroll Anita in the 21st Century Program in part so that she could have a one-on-one tutor. The family was to be referred to an agency for counseling that might help Anita to better cope with the family tragedy.

The first session with the family in late February of 2005 began at Family Focus before moving to the Robbins home. Like many poor black students in Evanston who have working parents who cannot afford after-school childcare, Anita goes to the Family Focus center, which is a converted school building, while she awaits her grandmother. This day she worked for some time with an assigned tutor on her social studies and math assignments, and the staff person noted that she is easily distracted and lacks focus. She preferred to listen to music, talk with friends, make plans for the next day, and discuss a boy with whom she is "in love." When her grandmother arrived, she, her sister, and the staff person went to the grandmother's home, and almost immediately Anita and her sister argued over popcorn. The first observer pointed out that Anita typically prepared her own dinner, and that this was often junk food. This day her grandmother prepared dinner and the staff person convinced Anita to wait until after dinner to eat the popcorn. Her grandmother had tried without success to stop the altercation between Anita and her sister, which they later indicated was an effort to gain the attention of the staff person, whom they both knew fairly well.

Later that evening, Anita had still not completed her homework nor eaten her dinner. The next meeting took place 6 weeks later at the family home with a caseworker not connected with this research present. There was no quiet, uncluttered space in which Anita could do her homework, and her grandmother told the staff person that she was happy that the two girls would not have to testify in a court case that would certainly have been traumatic for them. Ms. Robbins never asked about school or homework, and dinner had not been started by 8 p.m. She is very concerned with Anita's education and seems prepared to fight for what she thinks they need. Still, she does not seem capable of giving Anita what she needs from her grandmother. The staff person indicated that Anita had completed an assignment notebook that helped keep the easily distracted young girl on task, but that her grades had not improved.

By the next month, the end of the academic year, Anita's grades had improved, according to the staff person. She wrote, "There have been great improvements in [Anita's] road to academic excellence." She now had a quiet place at home at which to do homework, and was becoming more focused. The staff person noticed that Anita was a very good dancer and believed that she should become involved in dance as an extracurricular activity. This was suggested to her grandmother, who promised to inquire about it over the summer. A tutor has been arranged for Anita 3 days a week to begin in the fall, but over the summer she was asked to continue to write in her academic journal focusing on her goals for the sixth grade. The staff person noted, however, that Ms. Robbins has little confidence in Anita's succeeding in a mainstream environment.

While part of this lack of confidence relates to a distrust of the school system, it also suggests a relatively low opinion of her granddaughter's ability, which is, of course, not good for Anita's self-esteem. The young lady is now in counseling to help her cope with issues in her personal life that relate to the traumatic experience mentioned earlier.

The next meeting with the family took place in the grandmother's home in the fall of 2005, and the staff person noticed "that things were different." Anita's room was now clean and uncluttered, and she now had a desk in her room at which she could do her homework. Still, she devoted over an hour that day to watching the television, suggesting that neither she nor her grandmother really understood the importance of that work and the need for avoiding distractions, or that they understood the need for time management or delayed gratification. Ms. Robbins had not arranged the dance activity, and the staff person again noted that Anita perhaps needs such an activity to help her deal with her very high energy level. Anita indicated that she dances because she feels creative, but there has been no effort to help her explore this creativity, despite several attempts to have Ms. Robbins respond to this creativity in a positive manner. Middle-class parents tend to help their children "cultivate" their talents (Lareau, 2003), and Ms. Robbins has not done this despite the suggestions of the staff person. The intervention has not managed to help Ms. Robbins understand the importance of this approach.

On the other hand, it may be that Ms. Robbins believes that dance lessons or even dance opportunities would cost money that she does not have. However, in a largely middle-income community such as Evanston, there are opportunities to have Anita involved in dance that would either be gratis or subsidized. Ms. Robbins would need to seek them out, but they are available. Middle-class parents find the opportunities that will benefit the growth and development of their children. Most poor parents do not, and their children often suffer as a result.

Ms. Robbins has also not yet learned to work with Anita on her homework, or to look over that work for mistakes, preferring to pay little attention to this work, and therefore failing to send to Anita the signal that she cares enough about this work to pay attention to it. This devalues Anita's education, despite her often stated belief that it is important to her that Anita perform well in school. The staff person again mentioned to her that this involvement with Anita and her schoolwork was very important, and was assured that a change would be made soon. The staff person stressed that at least 30 minutes a day should be devoted to Anita's homework, with Ms. Robbins working with her for the entire 30 minutes. We were not able to determine that this change took place because that was the last visit to the home. A last-minute scheduling change by Ms. Robbins prevented another visit.

The final visit with Anita took place at Family Focus, and the staff person indicated that Anita was very active, as usual, and did no homework when she should have been doing that work. She talked with friends, sang, and danced rather than work on her schoolwork. The staff person finally suggested to Anita that she attempt to do what she could before her tutor arrived, but apparently Anita wanted the staff person to simply provide her answers to her homework questions. The staff person concluded after working with Anita that she could indeed do the work, but that she needed to focus and avoid distractions. Anita apparently "feeds off the slightest attention from others." Her constant talking, singing, and dancing gets her the attention that she craves. This is the case for each of the four young people observed so far.

This may also be the challenge for those concerned with the education of poor black students. There are so many things in their lives about which they may feel bad and so many things that suggest to them that they have little value. So many people pay little attention to them, and so much of the attention paid to them is negative that almost any positive attention is sought. Remember, students need high self-esteem in order to deal with the reality that they will often be wrong in school. They will say the wrong things, have incorrect answers, and if they do not feel good about themselves, it will be difficult to handle the consequences of being wrong. The response may be to turn away from school. Anita has dance, and Jason has his craft and basketball. Ida has basketball. They all have activities that could be used to foster discipline, responsibility, delayed gratification, and higher self-esteem.

However, their parents/grandparents have not learned to take advantage of these opportunities in the way that most middle-class parents do. Indeed, they seek out these opportunities to help their children to develop and to feel good about themselves. We have not been able thus far to teach four families that this needs to be done, or perhaps, how to do it. Ms. Robbins was late arriving at Family Focus to pick up Anita, and Anita became angry with her. There was, however, no effort to discuss this with Anita, or to help her control her frustration. Another opportunity lost by both Ms. Robbins and our intervention effort. This was the final meeting of the intervention staff and the Robbins family.

During the 2005–2006 school year, Anita's grades were all Cs and Ds in her academic subjects, and As and Bs in fine arts, physical education, and drama. It is somewhat difficult to compare her grades during and after the intervention with those before because she was in the fifth grade when we began to observe and to work with her, and the Evanston Elementary School District does not award letter grades until the sixth grade. The intervention began while she was in the fifth grade and continued through the first grading period of the sixth grade. For that grading period she received Cs in language arts, reading, and social studies, and Ds in science and math. At the end of the year (after the intervention had ended) she received Ds in language arts, reading, social science, and math, and a C in science. It would be difficult to argue that Anita's grades had improved at all during our effort to help her grandmother learn to better prepare her for school.

Anita's grade report for the end of her fifth-grade school year indicated that she had trouble with self-control, responsibility, working independently, and turning her schoolwork in on time. Her sixth-grade report card suggested the same troubles. I certainly cannot argue that Anita has done better in school as a result of the intervention. Our attempts to help her grandmother learn to help her do better in school were unsuccessful, and Anita's behavior and attitudes have not improved. There may be some improvement in the future, but in the short term we have not made a difference in the classroom.

The second way that I wanted to measure the impact of these intervention efforts was in changes in the home environment that are related to better school performance, and of course this was done through comparing the observations of Anita's home environment before the intervention and after. This second set of observations began in late January of 2006 at Family Focus while the observer waited for Anita to be picked up by her grandmother. While some of the students worked on their homework, Anita practiced making up dance routines with one adult and two other students. The observer wrote, "[Anita] seems to love to perform and enjoys the attention she receives from dancing."

It is very clear that all of the students studied thus far have low self-esteem, and that the three girls in particular desperately crave attention. This need for attention is very problematic in schools, because it will often result in acting out to receive the needed attention. It is typically associated with low self-esteem and suggests that students will have difficulty dealing with criticism from a teacher, and perhaps even with offers of help from teachers, both of which occur almost every day in schools. While Anita can dance at home, at Family Focus, or on a playground and perhaps receive the attention that she very much seeks, she probably cannot do this in a classroom without stern comments from teachers. She may then find other ways to receive that attention, and almost all of the time these ways will result in behavior problems for her.

The next visit also began at Family Focus with the observer noting that Anita became "hyperactive" when she saw the observer. "She began dancing and playing around in an attempt to get my attention." The teacher at Family Focus indicated that Anita "does this all day," and that she had completed only one page of a three-page assignment from school in 1 hour, preferring to spend her time dancing and playing. The teacher laments her failure to get Anita to focus on her schoolwork. When Ms. Robbins arrived to pick up Anita and her younger sister, the observation moved to the Robbins apartment, which was described as small and cluttered. When asked where she slept, Anita replied that she generally fell asleep on the sofa while watching the television. It would be difficult to complete many homework assignments in that environment, and it is unlikely that many middle-class families would tolerate this whether they were middle-income or poor families.

The home life of students who perform well in school is highly structured and dedicated to the development of the child. The activities of the child are generally supervised by the parent, or at the least approved by the parent (Lareau, 2003), and falling asleep in front of the television on school nights is unlikely to be one of the approved activities. Anita showed the observer some photographs, and then played music while she showed the observer dances that she had choreographed. An 11-year-old choreographer is impressive, and this dancing ability may well be, as I have mentioned earlier, something that her grandmother or other concerned adults could build.

If Ms. Robbins convinced Anita that her dancing ability is special, and that she is special as a result, her self-esteem would certainly improve, laying the foundation for possible classroom improvement in both grades and behavior. However, it is Ms. Robbins who must understand this dynamic and be prepared to do something positive about Anita's ability and passion. The staff person working with the family suggested this, but nothing came of the suggestion. I find it difficult to believe that a middle-class family would not take advantage of this opportunity to develop the child's ability and sense of self.

Anita did no homework while the observer was in the home. Ms. Robbins arrived later with the younger sister, who had been crying because she had been accidentally left at Family Focus before her grandmother went back to get her. Instead of trying to calm the young girl who obviously had reason to be afraid and upset, Ms. Robbins "began screaming" at the child. Indeed, all of her communication with the girls "were in a loud screaming voice," not the calm, measured tones needed to comfort, reassure, and inspire children, nor the kind of adult behavior designed to teach children self-control so often used in middle-class homes. Ms. Robbins did order Anita to complete her homework, but Anita ignored her, preferring instead to talk on the telephone with a friend. Ms. Robbins informed the observer that Anita had a problem that made it difficult for her to focus, and that she was to have a prescription to help deal with this problem. She also mentioned that Anita was trying to deal with the aforementioned traumatic event, and that she no longer knew what to do with Anita.

When Anita realized that she was the topic of the conversation she began to rant and rave about how much she hated her teachers, how they were the cause of her poor performance, and that one white teacher was biased against black students. She then turned her attention to the television for the rest of the time. To protect the identity of this family, I will not detail either the cause of the stress that Anita faces or the "problem" that affects her. The traumatic event occurs all too often in poor communities, and is generally very difficult for poor, young children to comprehend or cope with. Suffice it to say that this young lady has serious issues, but efforts to get these under control are being made. Ms. Robbins is at a loss not just about how to deal with these issues, but also about what to do to better prepare Anita for school, despite our efforts to help her do these things. Still, there are very serious problems that this young lady faces, and we should not underestimate the impact of these problems on her behavior or performance in school. With little knowledge, resources, or experience, Ms. Robbins is at a disadvantage in responding to these problems.

However, it is still true that Anita is receiving help with these emotional problems, but not much help at home in dealing with her school problems. When Irving (1990) argues that black students do poorly in school because of their race, social class, and culture, he ignores the facts that not all black students perform poorly, that not all are poor (and some of the poor are middle class), and that there is really no one black culture. The reality is that public schools are and probably shall remain an "instrument of the mainstream culture" (Comer, 1993). Therefore, poor black students must find ways to negotiate that culture, and black and Latino parents need to find ways to help them become more successful at doing this. I see little or none of this in the Robbins household thus far.

The next visit with the Robbins family began at Family Focus, where a Black History Month concert was being held, and in which Anita's younger sister performed. Unfortunately, Ms. Robbins could not be there to watch since she had to work. This kind of scheduling conflict is a reality for many, if not most, poor families. While middle-income families typically plan their lives around the activities of their children, demonstrating in the process their support for them and the value of that activity, most poor families, even those that try to do the things that help prepare their children for school, lack that flexibility.

When the family and the observer arrived at the family apartment, the apartment was "extremely messy." "Food, candy wrappers, parts of toys were laying all over the floor." Both girls ate candy right away and threw the wrappers onto the floor. By all appearances both girls continued to sleep on the sofa in front of the television. Anita asked Ms. Robbins whether she had remembered to purchase something that Anita wanted for a school function the next day. When told that she had not, Anita became very upset and started to cry, to which Ms. Robbins replied, "Too bad." Anita then began to scream at her grandmother, yelling that Ms. Robbins was fat and ugly.

When Ms. Robbins yelled for Anita to leave the kitchen, she went into the living room and yelled to her sister that she was a "crack head." Anita then went into her bedroom and began to throw books at the wall, to tear the pages out of books, and then to throw anything that she could touch at the wall, explaining that it was better to take her anger out on things rather than on people. I give all of this detail because it is such a vivid example of much of the problems that are too often seen in the homes of many poor families, and in this one despite our efforts to help the grandmother help Anita. There is little impulse control, little delayed gratification, no discipline, no responsibility, and no self-control by either Anita or her grandmother. There was no discussion of the issue, no thinking about it. There were none of the attitudes or behavior that seem to characterize middle-class families and homes, and that are so valued by schools.

When Anita finally calmed down, she told the observer that Ms. Robbins had intentionally failed to purchase the item that she wanted because her grandmother did not care about her. Of course this was said in anger, but if Anita believes this at all, her behavior would be difficult to control. If she feels that her grandmother does not care about her, has no discipline, no self-control, low self-esteem, and cannot delay gratification, there is little chance that she can do well in school despite the efforts of the school staff, and apparently despite our efforts.

It seems that Ms. Robbins has a strategy, if I can call it that, for raising these children that can best be described as one of survival. In fact, during our initial interview with her, she indicated that she wanted Anita to feel "safe and secure," and "grounded." She just wants to keep them fed, clothed, and with a roof over their heads. Of course, she wants them to do well, but it is not clear that she believes she has the responsibility to do and to say the things that can lead to this outcome. It is her responsibility to keep them going.

This is not a strategy that will help prepare them for school, and we were apparently not able to help her to change that approach. There is little effort to help in the social, cognitive, or emotional development of the children. In fact, that development does not seem to enter her mind. This is a large part of what we wanted to change. Of course, there are obstacles in her way, serious obstacles, but she could still do her part, and she does not. By the way, Anita did no homework that evening either.

During the next visit to the Robbins home, the observer noted that Ms. Robbins speaks to the children "in a constant yelling tone." This is not the kind of quiet, orderly, structured home that I have observed in families of poor black and poor Latino students who do well in school, and we tried for some 7 months to change this. Anita ran to her grandmother at one point to hug her and say, "Love me, Grandma," one of the very few signs of affection that we see in this home, and perhaps a sign of how much affection Anita wants and needs, but does not receive. She spent the remainder of that evening watching the television and did no homework. Ms. Robbins did not ask one question about her schoolwork.

During the next visit, both girls screamed for the observer to play with them. These children need attention and affection very badly, and both of these characteristics are crucial in the development of positive self-esteem, which is of course critical for good school performance. Anita showed the observer a prize that she had won at school, and for which she was very proud. In many middle-class homes this award would be the cause of celebrations, celebrations that would help the child feel positive about himself or herself, to believe in his or her abilities. In this home, it goes unnoticed by Ms. Robbins. Anita spent this evening playing and dancing with her young cousin and sister while watching the television, and doing no schoolwork.

Ms. Robbins had indicated earlier in the evening that the teachers at the parent–teacher conferences told her that Anita was a bright student, but that she could not focus and does not want to put in the effort with her schoolwork. Anita was to receive help with the focus issue very soon, but Ms. Robbins apparently did not see the connection between what she does not do at home, and Anita's failure to do the schoolwork, again, despite our efforts to help her make the connection.

By the final visit, Anita had received the medical help that she apparently needed to help with the focus problem, but seemed embarrassed by this help. It seems that some adult needed to help her to better un-

derstand what she needed and why. Some adult needed to really talk
with her as opposed to talk down to her or to yell at her. Some significant adult also needed to give her the positive attention that she, like the
others discussed so far, so desperately needs. When the observer indicated that she was about to leave and that this would be her last visit,
both of the Terry girls draped themselves around her body and refused
to let her go. The observer, as has been the case in the past, provided
the attention that these children need and are willing to act out for. Unfortunately, this was not the observer's job. It is Ms. Robbins's job, but it
may have to be done by some outside agent.

I find it interesting that in the homes of the poor black and poor
Latino students whom I have observed in the past and who perform well
in school, the observer is almost invisible. The students are so busy with
their household chores or their homework that they hardly notice the
observers, and their parents, generally a mother, give them constant attention, direction, and praise. In Anita's home, as is the case for the
other three students observed to this point, the observers seem to be the
only source of attention for the students. I wanted to determine whether
this could be changed, and if so whether the change would affect school
performance. At this point, the picture is not really clear.

However, the discipline, self-esteem, and anger issues that were observed in the Robbins home when we first contacted Ms. Robbins are
still there. Anita still does no homework. She still does pretty much as
she pleases in the home. Instead of discussion, there is confrontation.
Ms. Robbins is still blaming others for Anita's poor school performance,
and she still provides little of the support, guidance, attention, and nurturance that Anita needs if she is to be successful in school. The apartment is no less cluttered and no more structured, and Ms. Robbins still
tends to yell at the children when she does communicate with them. So,
the home environment is little changed and still not conducive to good
school performance. Anita's grades have not really improved and neither
has her reported behavior. There is, on the other hand, little doubt that
this young lady has had to cope with two serious problems. There are
professional efforts to deal with both, but Ms. Robbins does not seem to
be able or willing to help Anita deal with them.

Poverty is a serious issue, and one of the problems. Poor parents must
learn to do the things necessary for their charges to do better in school

despite the poverty. But those who are really concerned with how poor nonwhite students perform in school must also be prepared to take on the problems that poverty presents. Ms. Robbins could not be supportive and attend a play in which the younger sister had a part. She was not able to pay her this attention because she had to work. In Ida Smith's home it was concern about paying the gas and light bill. Jason Green's mother had to worry about the loss of her job.

We wanted to determine whether we could teach the parents and grandparents to do some of the things done in middle-class homes that we know help to help the children do better in school. While I shall address the critical question of whether we have done this later, it has become clear that poverty presents issues and challenges that complicate this effort. Still, many poor nonwhite families have managed and continue to manage to overcome these challenges. It may not be that "easy" for others.

I need to point out here that at this point I have not seen any positive involvement in the upbringing of any of these children by a male. There was a male, a grandfather, present in only one of the three homes, and he did almost nothing. These are women playing the roles of mother and father. They must provide for the families, support the families, and find the time and energy to nurture the children. They must do it all, and this is not easy to do. Many poor black women manage to do this, but we may be asking too much of others.

⑦

JUAN LUIS MARTIENEZ

I believe that Lareau (2000) was correct when she wrote, "It is wise to have research projects that are intensive and small in scope" (p. 192). As a result, all of my research efforts that have centered upon the specific things poor nonwhite families do that influence the educational performance of their children have been relatively small and very intensive. One of the problems with this type of research, however, is that the researchers have very little control over the sample being studied. This is particularly problematic when those families being observed are poor, because poor families very often have crises that require them to change their lives very quickly, and thereby affect our research. Given that the samples are of necessity small, it is difficult then to replace the families, and simply not reporting on them is also a problem because it raises the question of possible manipulation of the data.

If there is a large random sample and 15% of those contacted refuse to participate in the survey, there is generally no harm done, and the data is analyzed and reported. However, when the sample is eight or nine and one or two families decide at some point to drop out or move and cannot be contacted, what should we do? I have elected to report and analyze the data that I have, understanding that what has happened with a particular family may well limit my conclusions. That is what has happened with the Martienez family, and to some extent with the Rosales family.

I have reported on the results of the first set of observations of the Martienez family. Juan Luis was then a 9-year-old third-grader at a Chicago school who had earned basically grades of D, and had problems with self-control, making independent decisions, completing tasks, and being courteous. He lived with his grandmother, her fiancé, and his three siblings. His grandmother has since married the fiancé, and she does not work. This makes this family different from three of the poor black families that we have already discussed, in that an adult is at home full-time and presumably has the time and energy to devote to child rearing and school preparation. On the other hand, it is the third of the five families reported on to have a grandmother raising the children. This means that an older adult is in charge, an adult now trying to raise a second generation of children. These grandparents are likely to have less energy, less stamina, and a weaker connection to the world of the children than the natural parents would have. Of course, this makes child rearing and school preparation more difficult for them and for the children.

In Juan's case, the curriculum focused upon helping his grandmother learn to provide and maintain a household structure that supported his homework, and help develop responsible behavior on his part. There was also a goal of providing support for Ms. Martienez in her role as a parent who is capable of setting limits and enforcing household rules. It appears that this is often a problem with grandparents, who have been finished with child-rearing obligations and now find that they need to take on these duties again. It is almost as though they are too tired to parent, and the grandchildren therefore do almost as they please.

The specific activities that were to take place in order to reach these goals included the following: identification of duties and household chores for which Juan would be responsible; identification of rude behavior on Juan's part and the establishment of consequences for that behavior; development of a system of rewards for positive behavior, setting standards and rules for the household; and finally, the development of standards and rules for the completion of homework. The Family Focus staff working with this family also thought that it was important to find a parenting group in which Ms. Martienez could participate that could help her to better grasp her responsibilities as a parent. They also wanted to help her enroll in an English as a Second Language class, given her limited grasp of English and Juan's need for mastery of English in school.

Before living with his grandmother Juan lived with his mother, and the grandmother indicated that his school performance had improved significantly since he had come to live with her. This suggests that the living situation with the mother was not particularly stable. During the next visit to the home, the staff person noted that the home was clean and well organized, and the interaction with Ms. Tajeda and her husband was "polite and comfortable." She went on to note, "The tone of voices was very tranquil," a far cry from the tone in Anita Terry's household. The parents/grandparents that agree to participate in our intervention effort are asked to sign a "contract," indicating that they are aware of the goals and objectives of the intervention, and they agree to participate in the process. Ms. Tajeda wanted help but did not want to sign the contract. She agreed that help was needed, but she did not want to get involved.

This is not unusual for poor families, because many of them have little or no knowledge of institutional behavior and therefore fear anything that appears to be "official." Ms. Tajeda acknowledged that she needed help and that Juan needed help to improve his reading, but she cancelled the next several appointments. She finally signed the contract after several attempts, but could not be reached at home either by telephone or in person. Finally, she contacted the Family Focus staff to tell them that Juan's mother had died a short time before in a tragic event witnessed by Juan. As was the case for Anita Terry, who was also affected by a tragedy that involved her brother and her parents, Juan was referred to a counselor.

This type of family tragedy will almost always affect the schoolwork of a child, and certainly has an impact upon this research. Ms. Tajeda was at that point struggling with the death of her daughter-in-law, trying to raise another generation of children, at least two of whom were also struggling with the tragic loss, and trying to deal with the issue of the guardianship of the children.

At one point, she told the staff person that she felt stressed and "desperate." In a telephone call a week or so later, she said that Juan Luis at times performed well in school and at times his performance was not as good. She also indicated that Juan Luis often did not want to obey her. The staff person had the impression that Ms. Tajeda did not want staff members to visit her, but a month later she did allow such a visit to her home and eagerly showed the staff member Juan's report card that indicated improved performance on his part. Apparently two of Juan's siblings had been placed by the government agency that deals with children and family issues with another family, and Ms. Martienez believed that they were receiving good care. Juan's father wants custody of the children, but only when he became "more stable." The staff person noted that Juan appeared "happy and relaxed" during this visit, and "was very attentive." She congratulated him for his improved school performance, and pointed out that he now followed direction and was "very polite."

During the final home visit, Ms. Tajeda informed the staff member that she had set aside a space for Juan's homework, but she also said that he did that homework while at the after-school program. While these two statements are not necessarily contradictory, it is not clear that the space is being used. Ms. Tajeda noted very serious and complicated childcare issues. There was a chance that authorities would place Juan with the family that had his siblings, causing him more disruption, and that she was caring for a nephew who was supposed to be with her for one day. However, the mother had not returned for a week to pick the child up.

All the rest of the contacts with the family were via the telephone. Were not able to spend much time with the family in the home, and were therefore not able to even try to implement much of the curriculum given that much of it centered upon changes in the home environment. This family was under a great deal of stress, and it is likely the case that Juan's school performance varied with that stress and the increased stability provided by his grandmother as time passed. It certainly is the case that Ms. Martienez had more important things with which to deal than our intervention at the time.

The tragedy with Juan's mother was reported in April of 2005, and by the end of the 2005–2006 academic year his grades were quite good. He received a C+ in reading and writing, a C in listening, an A in speaking, a C+ in research standards, a B in science, a B− in math, and showed improvement over the course of the academic year, probably as a result of the increased stability in his home life and the emotional distance from the event with his mother. It certainly was not the result of anything that we provided because although we tried, we were not able to intervene or to try to help Ms. Martienez to do more of the things known to help with school performance. Juan still had some behavior and attitude problems, but who would not, considering what he had to endure?

It is easy for those concerned with the academic performance of poor nonwhite schools to think that if we provide more money for schools or provide "better" teachers or if students would only try harder then these children will perform better. However, as we see with Juan and with Anita Terry, it is seldom that simple. I have often written and said that poor nonwhite students can perform well in school if the parents or guardians help with their homework, assign household chores that instill discipline and responsibility, encourage participation in extracurricular activities that do the same, maintain a quiet, ordered home environment, work to instill high self-esteem and internal control in the student, and teach the student to delay gratification, all other things being equal. Well, it is all too often the case that for poor nonwhite students all other things are not equal, and they often lack the emotional or experiential resources to respond in the same way that middle-income families may respond.

It is difficult for a parent or guardian to work on the development of critical thinking skills or to concentrate on engaging a child in discussion when the concern is the payment of the rent or the light bill, or whether you will even have custody of your grandson, or the welfare of his siblings who have been taken to another home. While some poor families manage to do the needed things, many more do not. Although some of those who do not simply do not care enough (even though almost all of them say that they care), others want to learn how to better prepare their charges. Unfortunately, they find that the pressures and the stress of the world in which they live get in the way. Schools cannot remove these pressures, and neither could we.

The second set of observations of the Martienez home began in January 2006 at the small apartment of Ms. Tajeda. Mary, the young cousin of Juan Luis, who accompanied the observer into the apartment and immediately resumed her homework on the kitchen table, greeted the observer. Juan Luis was in his bedroom watching television, and informed the observer that he had completed his homework in school. He began to tell the observer about a school talent show in which he was to dance and proceeded to show the observer "some moves" that he intended to use as a part of his dance routine.

Ms. Martienez told one of Juan's sisters, Sara, to complete her homework, and when she asked the observer for help, Juan informed Sara that the observer was there for him and not for his sister. It seems that all of the children with whom we have worked are starving for attention. This suggests a lack of confidence or low self-esteem, and I have yet to observe a parent or grandparent who seemed to understand this or to realize just how important self-esteem is for school preparation.

After watching the television for some time Juan accompanied an older brother into his bedroom. When three of the Martienez brothers emerged from the bedroom, they told their step-grandfather that they wanted to go out to play basketball and asked whether Juan could accompany them. When they told him where they intended to play, the step-grandfather gave permission for the older boys to go but indicated that Juan was too young to go because it was late and the gangs were dangerous in the area, especially after dark. Juan did not accept this very well, running to his room to sulk. His step-grandfather followed him and told him that it was rude to leave the observer. Clearly, there is some discipline and sense of responsibility in the home.

When the observer arrived for the next visit she was greeted by Sara, the younger sister, and then Juan, both of whom were playing outside of the apartment building. When Juan entered the apartment running, Ms. Tajeda told him that there was "no running in the house," another effort to maintain order and to establish discipline. When she asked Juan whether he had completed his homework, he again replied that he had in fact finished the work in school. Since Ms. Tajeda did not check that work she had no way of knowing whether that work was in fact completed. She did ask Juan whether he had practiced playing the drums, to which he replied that he had not, and she suggested that he should do that before doing anything else. Juan was not happy about this, but she told him that he needed to do this before going outside to play again. The scant attention to homework is problematic, but Ms. Tajeda does exert discipline and in her way was teaching Juan to delay gratification.

After a discussion with the observer about gangs, Juan played a CD and showed the observer a sweater that he said had gotten him into trouble because it had the word "hell" on it. He tried to explain that it was this word that caused him the trouble, but he refused to use the word, preferring to spell it out, before beginning his drum practice. Soon Juan and the observer went outside to play basketball and were joined by his sister Sara and one of her friends, whom Juan constantly chided for swearing when she did not play well.

During the next visit, Ms. Tajeda left to pick up Juan, who had band practice, from school, leaving the observer with Mary and Sara. During a conversation, Mary indicated that her school had no facilities for the handicapped but it did have "a whole lot of pregnant girls. That's all my school has." She went on to say that there were "freshmen, sophomores, juniors, and seniors" who were pregnant. A moment later Juan arrived and asked the observer whether she wanted to look at his science project, and when she replied that she did, he proudly showed the project to her. Mary was not pleased, indicating that he had been showing that project for a week. When Juan took offense, asking his grandmother to tell her to shut up, Mary said that he was behaving like a big baby. Juan continued to pout and to stomp his feet while holding onto his grandmother, while Mary continued to antagonize him, until Ms. Tajeda yelled at her to stop, before asking Juan whether he had any homework. When he said that he did not, she asked again. This time Juan stomped his foot and answered that he did not, but Mary said that he always says that he finishes his homework at school, but that he is lying.

Juan told Mary to shut up before his grandmother told the both of them to calm down. Juan stomped off angrily to his bedroom, but his grandmother followed and asked whether he was okay. He and the observer spent the rest of the evening watching the television in his bedroom.

I think that it is clear that Ms. Tajeda tries very hard to maintain the kind of home environment that should better prepare Juan for school. There is consistent discipline, and Juan must delay gratification. He is involved in an extracurricular activity, an activity that requires discipline and responsibility. She asks about homework, but does nothing to require that it is completed, let alone work with him on that work. There is no assigned place to do schoolwork, and the television is often on. The home is quiet, orderly, and structured, and she speaks to the children in quiet tones. At one point, Ms. Tajeda told Juan that she could check to see whether he had completed his homework at school because she talks with his teacher every day. If this is true—and it could well be given that she is a member of the Local School Council, or the quasi-governing body of the school—she is really an involved grandparent.

Although the home environment is not much changed from the year before, there was really no intervention that might have helped to change it. There was no consistent attention to Juan's self-esteem, and not much to his self-control, though it does appear that he is not simply allowed to do or say as he wishes. He acts out a fair amount, but he is, after all, a 10-year-old. Juan spends a lot of his time watching the television and playing outside. There is little discussion in the house, little that might foster critical thinking skills. There is no attention to reading in the house.

In some ways, the Martienez apartment is like many middle-class homes, and in some ways it is very different. Our efforts have little to do with the similarities given that we were not able to really work with the family because Ms. Tajeda was not often available. Like Anita Terry, Juan has experienced a very traumatic event involving a family member. However, based upon our second observations and his grades and reported school behavior, it appears that he has thus far handled that experience somewhat better. He had an advantage in that his home environment was somewhat more stable than Anita's. His grandmother did not need to work and therefore was available to be more supportive. She seemed to be more willing to take on the role of disciplinarian, and more capable of communicating with Juan in a more reassuring manner. He receives more attention from family members than does Anita.

Given what they have had to endure, it is impressive, to say the least, that they even try to do well, and it is not clear that Anita is really trying terribly hard. The stability and the attention serve Juan well, but there is work to be done in his household. While Ms. Tajeda pays more attention to Juan than most of the other parents or grandparents with whom we have worked pay to their charges, there is virtually no attention paid to the kind of development of skills that Comer (1993) indicates is needed or the cultivation or development that Lareau (2003) suggests is the cornerstone of middle-class child rearing.

These parents and grandparents seem to believe that their role is to provide the basic necessities for the children—food, clothing, and shelter—and so far we have seen very little attention to the development of self-control, thinking skills, ability to interact with others, ability to delay gratification, higher self-esteem, or the ability to negotiate conflict. While these are clearly not exclusively middle-income characteristics, in a number of the families with whom we have worked the sheer pressures of surviving and/or overcoming serious obstacles have made focusing upon child development very difficult despite our efforts to have these parents and grandparents do so.

⑧

JOSE ROSALES

Jose was in the 2003–2004 academic year a better student than most of the students with whom we worked. In fact, he received no grade below a C in reading, writing, listening, speaking, research methods, or math, and his grades in art, music, and physical education were Cs and Bs. He had problems in habits and behavior only with completing his homework and in exercising self-control. However, his teacher indicated that he needed to improve in three of the six reading areas, three of the four writing areas, and two of the five math areas. So, Jose is a decent student with few behavioral problems, but he needed to improve in several areas. Unfortunately, the family moved several times during our work with them, and we were not able to obtain the final grades of the 2005–2006 academic year, which would have allowed us to judge the success of the intervention with any change in his grades.

Ms. Roman was sufficiently concerned about Jose's education that she arranged to have him continue to attend the same school after the move as before, even though they were no longer in the attendance area of that school. We have the grades from the first grading period of that academic year and I shall discuss those grades a bit later. It might have been better to have Jose's final grades from that year, but as is often the case with poor families, they move quite a bit and it is sometimes difficult to maintain contact with them.

The curriculum for the Rosales family focused upon helping to support Ms. Roman in her parenting role, helping to arrange opportunities for Jose to become involved in extracurricular activities, increasing Jose's self-esteem and sense of responsibility, helping the family to better structure a home environment that would be more conducive to the completion of homework, and the implementation of a practice that would improve Jose's reading and writing skills. Ms. Roman speaks little English, and since this hampers her ability to deal with Jose's schoolwork, it was thought that the Family Focus staff should point her toward English as a Second Language classes, and that they should look into the possibility that Jose's homework instructions could be done in Spanish. The language barrier, though fairly common in some Latino communities, is often a problem for some families. It makes it difficult to communicate with some teachers, and may hamper the ability of a parent to even understand the homework, let alone to help with that work. The staff thought that it was necessary to try to help Ms. Roman deal with this barrier.

The work with the family began in February of 2005 with the explanation of the intervention to Ms. Roman and Jose by the staff person from Family Focus. As soon as that staff person explained what needed to be done in the home in order to enhance the chances of academic success for Jose, Ms. Roman turned the television off, and agreed to try to keep her very active younger son busy so that he would not interrupt Jose as he did his schoolwork. However, at the time of the next visit, both Jose and his mother were watching the television before they turned it off. Ms. Roman did discuss with Jose a plan to identify a certain area of their apartment to be used for his schoolwork, and told him that he could not watch the television unless he completed his homework. It appears that Ms. Roman says and does much of what is needed when the staff person is in the home. The question of course is what is done after that.

The staff person noted that Ms. Roman has a great deal of interest in helping Jose to perform better. I have found this high level of concern with the education of children to be fairly common among Latino families. However, the staff person also noted that Jose needs to be more honest with his mother about his homework. When the child speaks both English and Spanish, the parent speaks only Spanish, and most of the schoolwork and school information comes home in English, it is relatively easy for the student to mislead a parent where that schoolwork is concerned. I have observed this before (Sampson, 2004), and it was something that needed to be addressed in the Rosales home.

During the next meeting, Ms. Roman was given information that would help her make a study guide for Jose. This of course was designed to both provide the study guide, and also to involve Ms. Roman in Jose's education more than she had been involved. Ms. Roman indicated that she had identified a place in their small apartment for Jose's homework, and that she had made it clear to him that he was to devote at least one hour a day to that work, and to reading and writing. She also told the staff person that she had sent the active younger brother to Mexico for a time so that he would no longer interrupt Jose as he worked. Of course, the youngster would return, but the thought of limiting the distractions for Jose was important. Ms. Roman had also assigned Jose household chores that were designed to instill some discipline and sense of responsibility.

Jose had been enrolled in two after-school programs, one of which focused on helping with reading and writing and the other designed to help with his homework. While this suggests that Jose received quite a bit of help with his schoolwork, that help was not coming from Ms. Roman. So, she was not as involved with Jose's education as she might have been and needed to be. It is this kind of parental involvement that sends to the child the message that education is very important. During another meeting, Ms. Roman indicated that Jose needed a great deal of work with his vocabulary and pronunciation. So, she is at least attentive to Jose's educational needs. As is so often the case, however, with poor families the reality of poverty gets in the way of good intentions.

When the staff person asked Jose during the next visit why his report card had indicated that he often failed to complete his homework on time, he replied that he was often too tired to complete the work. Eight-year-old boys are rarely tired. Ms. Roman told the staff person in response to her question that Jose generally went to bed at 10 p.m., but that he would often wait for her to return from her job before going to bed, and this was much later. She wanted to find another job, a job that did not require her to work so late and allowed her to avoid working on weekends so that she could have more time with her young sons. She worked the only job that she could, and that job limited her time with her sons and made it very difficult for her to monitor Jose's activity or schoolwork.

Still, in June the staff person met in the apartment with Ms. Roman and his teacher. When the teacher was asked about Jose's academic level, she indicated that he had begun the school year at a low level but that he was doing much better at the time. Indeed, he was now pushing himself, and his behavior at school had also improved substantially. He had become more respectful, more polite, and more mature. It is of course difficult to attribute these positive changes to the intervention alone, and it may be that they are transitory. However, it is clear that Jose was doing better in school during the intervention than he was before, and that Ms. Roman was not only paying more attention to his education but also trying to do those things that might help him perform better. This suggests that the effort was beginning to work.

The next series of meetings with the Rosales family began in the fall of 2005, with the Family Focus staff person stressing to Ms. Roman the things that she needed to do to continue and enhance this academic improvement, and now Ms. Roman said that she was aware of those things. Now Jose becomes angry when it is late and he has not completed his homework, but the staff person explained that he must be given a set time for that work so that he would not finish so late. Ms. Roman also told the staff person during a subsequent conversation that she wanted to learn to speak English so that she could help with the children's homework. Clearly, she seems to know what she needs to do, and is prepared to do those things. That is progress.

During the final visit to the Rosales home, Jose said that he is now more relaxed because he does his homework after school while at the after-school program. This takes the time pressure off him at home. However, it also means that Ms. Roman is not as likely to be involved with Jose while he does that work, and is less likely to even know what that work is or whether it is actually completed. Ms. Roman worried aloud that Jose at times does not do as she says. This is not uncommon with young boys. The issue is just how she will handle the problem.

During the first marking period of the 2005–2006 academic year, Jose's grades were all either Cs or C−. He received a C in reading, writing, speaking, and math, and showed little in the way of behavior problems.

So, his grades were stable and his behavior acceptable. The intervention did not help him improve his grades, based upon the grades that were available to us, but remember that his teacher at the end of the 2004–2005 school year indicated that she had seen significant improvement in his performance. As I have indicated earlier, it may well be that improvements in grades will not be evident until some time has passed.

This is one of the primary reasons why I thought that it would be a good idea to do a second set of observations with the families. This allows us to determine whether there have been changes in the homes that have been associated with better school performance among poor nonwhite students. These observations of the Rosales began in February of 2006 at the Rosales's new one-room apartment. When the Family Focus staff person asked Jose about his most recent grades he replied that he had the report card with him, but Ms. Roman told the staff person and the observer that Jose had not shown her the report card; indeed, he had not mentioned the card to her. It is of course difficult for a parent to keep up with a child's school progress if the child fails to show the parent the report card. Some Latino students can get away with this because the parents do not speak English and the card comes home in English quite often. Since they cannot read the report card, they sometimes do not ask about it. Ms. Roman mentioned that she was thinking about moving yet again, and suggested that her employment situation was precarious.

During the next observation, the two boys took turns showing off their toy cars, while Ms. Roman cleaned the apartment. Jose emphasized that he played with the cars only on the weekend. During the week, according to Jose, he completes his homework, watches the television, and then goes to bed at 10 p.m. However, the observation took place on a weekday and he did no homework. Ms. Roman mentioned that she attends a trade school Tuesday through Saturday in addition to working. She plans to graduate soon and to own her own business. She noted that this would allow her to pick up her children from school and day care when she wants, and this would reduce her reliance upon others.

While the observer and Ms. Roman talked, the younger son "was tossing toys all over the place," which annoyed his mother and led to his being reprimanded. Ms. Roman attempts to maintain some discipline in the house, and she told the younger son that if he continued to act out he would "do a lot of writing tonight"—an apparent reference to the form of punishment that she uses with him. Indeed, when asked about this she replied that this was in fact punishment for him and Jose, but that she on occasion makes them stand facing the wall as punishment. This is of course not the kind of reasoned discussion that Lareau (2003) indicates is characteristic of middle-class families, but poor parents often do not have the time, energy, or knowledge to use this approach with their children, and it appears that our intervention with the Rosales family has not changed that.

Ms. Roman does what she needs to do to survive. She works to ensure that her two boys are clothed and fed, and that they have a place to stay. She does not work on the development of Jose or his brother, but she does make certain now that Jose has household chores. She does not seem to pay much attention to her role in the development of her sons' ability to delay gratification or upon Jose's self-esteem. She did not discuss school with Jose. Jose told the observer that he had not yet completed his homework as he watched the television, and Ms. Roman said nothing about this. At this point it does not appear that Ms. Roman does many of the things associated with middle-class households and school success.

She does some of them, and it does not appear that we have helped her do a lot more of them. Still, she has a difficult life trying to raise two boys on her own, work, go to school, and learn to speak English. We may have been asking a lot of her. She clearly wants to learn to speak English so she can better help her children, and she attends a trade school in order to try to carve out a better life for them as well.

The observer noted that Jose generally asks his mother for permission to do things around the house, suggesting discipline on his part, but when he completed some task she had asked him to do, she did not take the opportunity to compliment him, something that builds self-esteem. Both boys spend much of their time watching the television, and this was months after Ms. Roman immediately turned the television off when the Family Focus staff person told her that the television interfered with Jose's ability to do schoolwork. Apparently, that lesson did not sink in. In fact, the subjects of school and school preparation were only raised once or twice during the 5 weeks that these observations took place, and that was early in the time frame, suggesting that Ms. Roman wanted to say and do that which was expected of her. As the family became more comfortable with the second observer they resumed to their normal routine, and that seems to have not included much about school or about child development for that matter. Ms. Roman is very concerned that her sons exhibit good manners and are considerate of others, characteristics that Jose's teachers seem to see in him.

However, Ms. Roman does not discuss or show much interest in the things that seem to interest Jose. She does not pay attention to the ability of her children to learn to interact with others. Jose does a fairly good job of this primarily because he has been taught to be mannerly and considerate, but not because Ms. Roman is concerned with his ability to deal with others. She shows nothing to suggest that she is concerned with his ability to think, his self-esteem, or his schoolwork. Little about the household routine has changed since our initial observations, and this suggests that the intervention has had little impact. Jose did not need the attention provided by the staff person nearly as much as some of the other children involved in this research, and as a result did not seem to benefit as much from that attention. Ms. Roman gives both of her sons positive attention routinely, but she does not translate that attention into attention to Jose's schoolwork.

Jose is being raised in a way that will allow him to be a student who causes little trouble for a teacher, and that will permit him to do a decent job in school, but the values, attitudes, and ways seen in his home are not really those of the middle class or of public school, and we were not able to significantly change that situation. Ms. Roman was in the process of learning to speak English and changing her job, both things that would permit her to become more involved with Jose's education were she to decide that this is what she should do on a consistent basis.

The home is still relatively quiet and orderly, but there is still no focus on a place for Jose to do his schoolwork, were he to do any at home. The home is still orderly, Jose is still disciplined, and Ms. Roman is still relatively calm with the children, all characteristics of higher-achieving poor nonwhite students. These characteristics were in place before our intervention. I have, however, not seen the changes that we set out to facilitate. There is still little engagement of Jose by his mother, no evidence that Jose is involved in any extracurricular activity or that specific hours have been set aside for homework after the staff person was no longer in the home. In short, this is another case in which the intervention has apparently not made much of a difference that we can see at this point. Since Jose was an average student it may be the case that not much was required, that is if average is acceptable.

The truth is though that I do not see many of the characteristics of higher-achieving students either before or after our intervention efforts. The question still is whether this is the result of any shortcomings of that intervention or of the family situation or of a relatively short time frame in which we expected to see the results of that effort. Of course, it could be all of these. That is probably the main concern with this type of research.

9

FEDERICO AND JOSE LUIS VILLAR

When we conducted the initial observations in the fall of 2004, Federico was a 9-year-old fourth-grader and his brother Jose Luis an 8-year-old third-grader who both attended the same Chicago school attended by the two other Latino students involved with this research. They both received average grades and displayed few behavioral or attitude problems, and neither believed that education was important. The curriculum developed by the Family Focus staff had as its objectives providing the parents support in assuming greater responsibility for the education of their children, the provision of opportunities for the development of increased confidence and self-esteem in both boys, and raising the boys' reading and writing skills. The staff believed that helping the parents enroll in parenting classes, establishing rules in the house for homework, encouraging the parents to offer verbal support for things that interest the boys, and to become involved in their schoolwork would help meet these goals. They also wanted to encourage the parents to become involved in school activities and the boys to become involved in extracurricular activities, to teach the family members to compliment one another, to help the parents identify household chores for the boys, and to refer both boys to the 21st Century Program.

For the most part, these goals and the activities designed to meet the goals reflect the belief that the Villar family needed help in beginning to think and act more like the families of poor nonwhite students who do well in school, families that themselves think and act much like middle-class families. These are activities designed to foster: discipline; responsibility; higher self-esteem; more parental involvement with school and with schoolwork; a quiet, orderly home environment conducive to homework; and the ability to delay gratification. The intervention meetings with the family began in February of 2005, and the staff person assigned to the family worked with the mother, Ms. Sanchez, to assist her in helping both boys. The initial meetings centered upon explaining the intervention process, and both boys and Ms. Sanchez were "positive" and enthusiastic. A place in the home was identified that was to be set aside for homework, and Ms. Sanchez and both boys were told that the area needed to be quiet, something not easily accomplished when there are six children in the house. Ms. Sanchez agreed to enroll in an English as a Second Language course in order to be a position to help her sons with their homework, which was often in English, a language Ms. Sanchez is not very comfortable with.

When the staff person arrived at the home for the third visit, Jose Luis was watching the television, but turned to his homework after the staff person arrived. Ms. Sanchez indicated that she had contacted Jose's teacher and been told by the teacher that Jose was making progress in his class and in getting his homework in on time. Federico was doing his homework when the staff person arrived, and continued with that homework while the staff person and Ms. Sanchez talked, primarily about the ESL class. In fact, he did not want to be interrupted while he worked in his bedroom. According to the staff person, Federico "has taken his responsibilities very seriously" and really wants to improve his school performance. It may be that the attention and focus is just what he needs in order to do better in school. Indeed, by the second month of the intervention, Ms. Sanchez reported that Federico was doing better in school according to his teacher, with whom she had recently met. In fact, the teacher had suggested that Federico did not need extra help. Remember that one of the goals was to have the family become more involved with the school, and it appears that Ms. Sanchez has begun to do that. On the other hand, Jose Luis asked the staff person for help with his homework rather than his mother. The staff person helped with part of the work, but asked him to do the rest. She went on to ask him to write and to show how much he knew of his multiplication tables.

Thus, in the case of Jose Luis, the staff person played the role that should have been played by Ms. Sanchez. If, however, Ms. Sanchez learned from this example then the work with Jose will have been appropriate. In May when the staff person met with Ms. Sanchez, she told her again how important it was for her to review Jose's homework everyday, how important it was to ask him to read and write everyday, and how important it was to have this done in a quiet place. Ms. Sanchez reported that Jose's grades had improved according to his teacher, and that he would be attending summer school as well as tutoring classes. Federico was also improving, but was not at home during this visit.

He was at home during the next visit, and was happy that his teacher had informed him that he had passed to the next grade. Clearly, Federico had low educational expectations if just passing a grade made him happy. Ms. Sanchez was happy as well because Federico's teacher had told her that he was doing well in class and that he had improved "a lot." This says two things: Ms. Sanchez is now in touch with the teacher, and the intervention at the least coincides with and may well influence this improvement. Jose Luis was also informed that he passed to the next grade, in his case, the fourth grade, and Ms. Sanchez was told that he too was doing better at the end of the academic year than at the beginning. Ms. Sanchez indicated that she wanted both boys to attend summer school, suggesting her concern for their educational progress and her willingness to do things to help them do better. It is noteworthy, however, that as is the case for many poor parents, she seems to expect others—in this case, summer school—to make the difference. She does not yet seem to understand her role in this process. Before leaving, the staff person told Ms. Sanchez to have the boys practice their multiplication tables over the summer, and had them write and read her a story. She noted that they both did "much better" than they did when she first met with them.

The boys were not able to attend summer school after all because the school was too far and they could not afford the transportation. In the fall the staff person met with the family and again emphasized to Ms. Sanchez that she needed to ask about and review homework every day, and that it was her responsibility to guide the progress that her sons should make. The staff person noted that Ms. Sanchez had yet to attend the ESL classes that would help her better understand the schoolwork that her sons brought home and to better communicate with the school staff. Ms. Sanchez works full-time and studies to master a skill that would allow her to obtain a better-paying job that might allow her more time with her children as well. This leaves her little time for ESL classes that might help her to help the children. This is a very difficult choice that is rarely faced by middle-income parents but often by the poor.

At the end of the 2005–2006 academic year, both Federico and Jose Luis were doing above average in terms of grades, and neither had any significant behavior problems. Federico received a C in the Reading Initiative, a C in writing standards, an A in listening standards, a C in speaking, a B in research, a C in math, a B− in science, and an A− in social science. His teacher wrote that he was a "pleasure" to teach, and that he was "responsible" in his behavior. Juan Luis had a C in the Reading Initiative, a C− in writing, an A in listening, and Cs in the other subjects. His teacher wrote that he was "a nice and quiet student" who was developing in all subjects. These students were doing fairly well in school when we first began to work with their mother, at least compared to the other students with whom we worked, and were doing a bit better when we completed that work.

Were there differences in the home environment or in what Ms. Sanchez did and did not do that could be related to the intervention? To try to answer this question, we observed the two boys and their family a second time beginning in January of 2006, with a different observer for each boy. One of the observers noted that television sets were on in three different rooms of the house during his first visit, and that Federico watched one in his room off and on. He also indicated that Federico was very responsive to his mother and quite obedient. When asked about homework, Federico said that he had spelling homework to do, but that he would do it later.

Neither parent asked any of the children about school or about homework, and neither parent really discussed anything with any of the children. Both boys were seen as shy by the observers, and not really comfortable with non–family members. While these characteristics may suggest that they will not cause teachers any difficulty and therefore be seen as "good" students, they also mean that they are unlikely to question or to probe most adults. This is not particularly conducive to higher achievement in school.

During another visit, the observer pointed out that Federico was allowed to watch a television show containing "graphic violence and sex" while his mother watched the show and said nothing to him about what he watched. He again said that he had homework, but did none of the work. After both of his parents left the house, he watched the television in the living room while three older siblings watched a television in another room. The lives of the children seems to center around television sets, while Mr. Sanchez focuses on his work and Ms. Sanchez on household chores. No one pays much attention to learning or preparing the two boys for learning. An older child has been very ill, and there was a great deal of concern about his well-being.

During another visit, Federico played a video game, watched the television, or played another game, while occasionally responding to his mother's directions to help her. The older brother was very ill, and given that he rarely left the sofa, the illness was apparent to all. It was not clear that the family was in a position to provide the needed care. His condition deteriorated during our observations and seemed to worry Jose Luis quite a bit. With the stress caused by this condition and the constant noise of the television sets, the home was not at all conducive to schoolwork or to much discussion about school or anything else for that matter. Neither Juan Luis nor Federico did any homework at any time during the 2 months of our observations. Neither parent asked either of them about school. Neither parent engaged them in any discussion about their day or concerns or interests. Neither parent said or did anything that might promote higher self-esteem or the ability to delay gratification. Neither child causes their parents any trouble, and they seem to be largely ignored as a result.

About 2 months after these observations began, the older brother died. During the final visit to the house Federico watched the television and played a game, while Ms. Sanchez, as usual, prepared dinner. One observer wrote, "It's unfortunate, but this family has so much on their plate that I do not blame them for not having the time to worry about their children's education. I am not saying (that) it is correct to neglect the education of a child, but when a mother is struggling to put food on the table and provide a warm bed for her children she has no time to worry about whether or not homework was done."

This statement reflects the reality not only of the life of the Sanchez family, but of several of the families that we have observed. While I have studied a number of poor nonwhite families in which the students do well in school, it is true that for the most part they have not had to cope with the kind of issues and concerns faced by the Sanchez family, or the Terry family, or the Tajeda family. These families face problems caused by and/or exacerbated by poverty. The Sanchez family does not seem to value education very much, and our intervention did not seem to change the household dynamic very much. It is true, however, that the ill son was not in the home at the time of the initial observation. His presence had an impact on the family dynamic. Still, there was no more attention to schoolwork or helping with that work. In fact, at one point, 10-year-old Federico was told that he would have to help his father with his manual labor job. Nor was there any more concern for the self-esteem of the two boys or for their ability to delay gratification. Nor was there any real discussion with the boys or any apparent concern for their development, or for their ability to relate comfortably with adults.

The boys tended to avoid eye contact with adults, a characteristic that Lareau (2003) identifies with the poor, but that I would associate with the non–middle class. The characteristics of middle-class homes that positively influence educational achievement seen often in middle-income households, and at times in the homes of poor nonwhites (Clark, 1983; Sampson, 2002, 2004; Tapia, 2000), were not much in evidence when we began work with the Sanchezes in the fall of 2004 or when we concluded that work in the spring of 2006.

When the staff person responsible for trying to help Ms. Sanchez help her sons do well in school was present, both she and the boys did some of the things that they were asked and expected to do. However, when left alone they generally did not. It is, however, very difficult to know the impact of the ill sibling on the family's ability to do these things.

10

CHANGING CLASS: WHAT HAVE WE LEARNED?

I set out to determine the extent to which poor nonwhite families with children doing poorly in school could be taught the things that they needed to change in order to better prepare their children for the educational experience. In effect, I wanted to determine whether we could help poor parents who behaved like non–middle-class parents to behave more like middle-class parents despite their poverty. Some poor nonwhite parents seem to have many of the values, beliefs, and behavior patterns of their middle-income counterparts, despite their lack of money. Given that for the most part, all things being equal, their children do quite well in school, the question was whether we could help others become more like the parents of successful children. Ultimately, of course, the issue was whether this model could be helpful in narrowing the education gap that exists between some poor nonwhite students and many middle-income white students.

There are a number of other intervention models designed to help parents better connect with schools in order to improve the performance of students generally, and of poor students in particular. The two most notable of these efforts are the Comer model and the Epstein model. While each model seeks to involve parents in school-parent partnerships, they are both in reality focused on changing or improving schools and see parental involvement as key to that process. The intervention model that I have laid out and tried to assess is by contrast designed to attempt to change families themselves, and not schools directly. It is not that I believe that most of the schools serving poor nonwhite students are doing what they should as well as they should. Rather, since I have found that some poor nonwhite students manage to do well in school while others much like them, and sometimes attending the same schools, do poorly, the question for me became why some and not others. Why is it that some poor nonwhite families do the things that need to be done, have the values, beliefs, and behaviors that help their children perform well—the mainstream or middle-class values, beliefs, and behavior—while others do not? The next question then became, can some families be taught to emulate the successful families?

Writing about school staff, Comer (1993) suggested that his efforts were designed "to improve their attitudes and behaviors, which, in turn, improved student and parent attitudes and behaviors" (p. 310). He designed a program that involved school staff and parents in an effort "to change schools." Thus, the focus was not so much on changing parents in order to help them better prepare their children for school as on involving parents in the effort to change schools. He developed a Governance and Management Team made up of 12 to 14 people that included parents, teachers, professional support staff, and nonprofessional support staff and led by school principals. The team was to develop a plan for school change, and since it involved parents it was thought that those parents would feel empowered and therefore to better deal with the schools.

Parents were also to be involved as school volunteers and in helping school staff carry out other school activities. The belief was that this kind of involvement would help parents understand what they needed to do in order to help their children do better in school. The main problem with this approach was that it relied largely upon self-selection, and was therefore likely to have parents who were more likely to do the right things at home than those who were not. The parents who feel confident enough to volunteer to help at school functions or to serve with professionals on the Governance and Management Team are unlikely to be the kind of parents or grandparents that we observed in the present study, and it is these parents whom we most need to reach and to help. It also relies heavily upon the good intentions of professional staff, especially school principals, and there is good reason to believe that these intentions are not always so good.

The Comer model is one approach, and given that it focuses on schools and fairly traditional parental involvement, it is unlikely that it will help many poor parents to adopt the values, beliefs, and behavior seen in many middle-class homes known to be associated with higher school performance. It may, however, help change schools that serve the children in these homes, and that would be a very good thing. My focus has been on changing parents and not on changing schools, though I realize that schools often need to change. I will leave that to Comer and to Epstein.

Epstein and her colleagues at the Johns Hopkins University formed the National Network of Partnership Schools (NNPS) "with the goal of providing school leaders with the knowledge and technical assistance to build effective relationships with parents" (Lareau, 2000). So, this model is also aimed to a significant degree at improving schools, though it does seek to both involve and to change parents to a more significant degree than does the Comer approach. What the NNPS refers to as the "School Model" is implemented by an Action Team that is to some degree much like the Comer Governance and Management Team. The Epstein approach does, however, seek to involve the broader community in the school change process, and has six very clear types of parental involvement, some of which are similar to those laid out in the Comer model, and some focused much more specifically on trying to change families in ways that I have explored (Epstein et al., 2002).

One of the types of parental involvement, for example, seeks to "help all families establish home environments to support children as students" (Epstein et al., 2002, 14) Another is to "provide information and ideas to families about how to help students at home with homework and other curriculum related activities, decisions, and planning"(Epstein et al., 2002, 14). While the involvement also includes parental volunteering and involvement in school decision making, as does the Comer model, it clearly attempts to change what families do at home in an effort to help better prepare children for school. I have been much more concerned with the parenting skills, the home conditions, and the involvement of parents with the schoolwork of the children in those families, largely because my research (Sampson, 2002, 2003, 2004) and that of others (Bempechat, 1998; Clark, 1983; Tapia, 2000) suggests that these are the things that help explain why some poor nonwhite students do well and others do poorly in school.

The focus on schools makes sense for school personnel and for most policy makers. We change schools in large part because we can, and not necessarily because those changes have made much difference for many poor nonwhite students. Quality preschool education makes a positive difference for many poor students, as do significant reductions in class size, but both are costly. Many middle-income white taxpayers are reluctant to pay more in property taxes to support changes that appear to mainly benefit poor nonwhite students, despite the reality that such improvements will help us all. The family-centered and the school-centered approaches are not at all mutually exclusive. Indeed, they should both be pursued.

Of course, there are a host of other efforts to intervene in the educational process in an attempt to help poor students perform better. It is not my purpose to review or evaluate those efforts here, particularly since for the most part those attempts have centered on schools themselves as opposed to parents and homes. Given my belief that the parents and the homes are the keys to the success of attempts to improve the academic performance of poor nonwhites, I focus on the parents and the homes. Irving (1990) and Dyson (2005) seem to reject this approach and label it as an example of the cultural deficit model. That is, as I have indicated above, they believe that efforts to help black parents change their behavior, beliefs, and attitudes in such a way that they might better prepare children for school are based upon a belief that there is something wrong with or inferior about those attitudes, beliefs, and behavior—about what they believe is black culture.

I do not attempt to help "black parents." Rather, I attempt to help only those poor nonwhite parents who have children performing relatively poorly in school. I cannot state often enough that not all poor black or poor Latino children are underachievers. Irving, Dyson, and most others overlook this reality and lump all black children together, not even bothering to make the distinction between poor black children and middle-income black children. Irving does acknowledge that it is important for parents to play the role of "teachers in the home," supervising the curriculum and talking with their children about graded papers and assignments due, as well as reading to their children and monitoring their television watching.

This is precisely what I wanted to try to help parents learn to do consistently, and it is not at all an indication of a belief that anyone is deficient. It is based upon the reality that public schools require students to exhibit certain values, attitudes, and behavior in order for them to do well, and that it is the responsibility of parents to make certain that children have the requisite characteristics.

It is interesting that Irving lauds the work of Clark (1983), yet writes about cultural deficits. Clark's work clearly examines the characteristics of high- and low-achieving black students, their parents, and their homes and suggests that parents can be taught to do many of the things that are routinely done in the homes of higher-performing poor black students. These values, beliefs, and behaviors are not deficits, and certainly not cultural. Folks tend to respond to the conditions under which they live, and for many poor nonwhites, the economic and social conditions of their lives often cause them to respond in ways that are not only not prized by most public schools but are also not useful in those schools. For many blacks, there is the added problem of racism, both individual and institutional.

Poor parents have concerns and worries that take precedence over reading to the children. Single black mothers need to work, provide for the home, and still have the time and energy to consistently praise their children for small accomplishments. Latino grandmothers faced with the responsibility of raising a second family must figure out ways to overcome their fatigue and worries. They must teach young children to delay gratification, all the while concerned that they may not even have the children much longer.

I am not at all suggesting that the adaptations that poor people make to their environments are deficits. In fact, these adaptations often show the strengths of those families. In some cases, however, as shown by Ogbu (1978), Clark (1983), Sampson (2002, 2004,), Lareau (2000, 2003), and Comer (1993), some of the characteristics that result from the adaptations are at odds with the "mainstream culture" about which Comer writes or the middle-class ways about which Lareau (2003) writes. In these cases, it makes sense to try to determine the extent to which some of these parents can be helped to change their beliefs, values, and behavior in a way that allows them to do more of the things done in the homes of poor nonwhite students who do well in school.

My concern was not with the traditional notion of parental participation in education: parent–teacher councils, school volunteer efforts, and attendance at school functions. My focus has been mainly on the home and the parenting skills. I do believe that it is important for children to be involved in extracurricular activities to foster discipline and responsibility, and that it then makes sense for parents to try to be supportive of those activities, though that is sometimes not easy for single working mothers. I agree with Lareau (2003) that while social class is important in the discussion of academic success, "it is not determinant." As I have stated before, I think that many poor folks are middle class in their beliefs, attitudes, and some of their behavior, and all others things being equal, their children can and often do fare well in school. I have enough faith in the others to believe that some of them can be shown what they need to do in order to help their children perform better, especially given that almost all poor nonwhite parents indicate that education is very important to them.

It is this type of help or assistance that I wanted to provide in this research, but the major goal of the research was to determine whether and to what extent this approach could be successful. That is, could it result in positive changes in the parenting skills of poor nonwhite parents, in the grades and school behavior of students, and in the home environments of the families studied? While there are a number of variables that strongly influence school success, families are almost always at the center of the discussion of academic achievement. Can students be successful without supportive, nurturing, caring, attentive, families? Of course, some can (Lareau, 2003). Can students be successful without parents teaching them to delay gratification or to believe in their abilities? Probably, some can. Can students be successful without parents or guardians providing a quiet, orderly, structured home environment or checking on their schoolwork? Perhaps. However, we know that the poor nonwhite students who have these things in place do significantly better in school than those who do not.

It makes sense then to try to determine whether we can successfully help others to make the needed changes, for if that can be done, it has significant implications not only for efforts to help poor nonwhite students perform better, but also for the research on school success. The focus might well then shift from schools, almost exclusively, to both families and schools. The kind of focus on the cultivation and development of children generally seen in the homes of middle-class families is often very different from the focus on surviving everyday life so often seen among many, but not all, of the poor, and public schools, as I have indicated, value well-developed and "cultivated" students. They value students who can consistently control their frustrations, delay gratification, and are internally controlled. They value those who have high self-esteem, who can interact with others, think critically, and are disciplined and responsible. They value students who come to class prepared to learn.

Research clearly shows that some poor nonwhite parents do develop these characteristics in their children, and for the most part those children do well in school. The research also shows that the parents of the successful poor nonwhite students provide a quiet, orderly, structured home environment, ask about schoolwork consistently, and involve themselves in the schoolwork of their children. These characteristics and behaviors are what I call middle-class characteristics, though I cannot overemphasize that they are not middle-income characteristics because they are not really unique to middle-income families.

The intervention was designed to foster more middle-income behavior, values, and beliefs among poor nonwhite families with students doing poorly in school, and if the measure of success of the intervention is significant and consistent improvement in academic performance, I would say that the success was spotty. If the success is to be measured by changes in the home and family dynamic as determined by fairly long-term observations in the homes, I would have to believe that the results were negative, at least during the time that we were in the homes, though there were some positive changes. However, two things were consistently found during this work: for a number of the families involved, the effects of poverty were so great that academic performance really could not be a high priority; and a number of the young people studied were so starved for positive attention that a little bit of that attention seemed to make a difference in their school performance.

Kendra Allen, a young black student in Chicago, improved her grades after our efforts to help her mother change herself and the home environment in order to assist Kendra. She improved her school behavior as well. However, the household dynamic did not improve, and her mother did not consistently change what she did and did not do in order to better prepare Kendra for school. Kendra was one of the students literally starved for positive attention. In fact, she was required to pay a great deal of her attention to her newborn sibling. Because our almost 2 years of efforts in her home gave her that attention, that focus on her, it is quite likely that this had a fair amount to do with the improvement in the grades and school behavior. In terms of policy, this suggests that things could be done to help her that do not include the type of intervention tried here because others could indeed provide that needed attention.

Ida Smith, another black student in Chicago, also did better in school as measured by reports of her behavior, but her grades improved and then regressed. Unlike Kendra, Ida did receive positive attention from family members. The household structure and dynamic did not change. Jason Green, the young black student from Evanston, did better in school, but the home environment did not change much, and Jason was involved with several programs designed to help him perform better in school. It may be that it was the impact of these programs that helped him improve his grades, but it is also true that Jason was another of the students who really needed positive attention, and he received that from our efforts.

Anita Terry, another black student from Evanston, had serious behavioral issues when we began to work with her family, and she had the same issues when we completed the work. There was apparently no real improvement in her academic performance or changes in the home environment. Her grandmother yelled at the children in the home when we began to try to help her, and she yelled when we completed the work. There was no more structure in the home, no more attention to schoolwork. There was no more attention to the development of higher self-esteem or discipline in Anita from her grandmother.

Juan Luis Martienez had his grades improve during the course of our intervention efforts. However, we actually were unable to help his grandmother very much given that she was not available. The home environment had some of the characteristics of many middle-class homes when we began observing the family, and had many of the same characteristics when we reobserved the family. Thus, it appears that not much had changed, including those characteristics that needed to change.

The intervention had little impact, as far as we were able to measure it, on the grades or on the family or home environment of Jose Rosales. His mother, Ms. Roman, does give him positive attention, but she paid no more attention to his schoolwork after our intervention than she did before. Since she speaks very little English, it is difficult for her to help with his schoolwork or to read to or with Jose. The brothers Federico and Jose Luis Villar were doing fairly well in school before our efforts, and were doing slightly better after those efforts, and neither had behavioral problems before or after the intervention. So, the intervention may have helped the school performance a bit, but the home environment did not change as a result of our efforts.

Overall then, it appears that the intervention had some success and some failure if success is measured by school grades and behavior and changes in the home. The families that we worked with faced problems and issues that as I have indicated earlier made focusing on school very difficult, and without doubt affected the outcome of our intervention efforts. One observer noted that three siblings of the student with whom we were working appeared to be members of a street gang. One adult in one of the homes did not want the young student to go out after a certain time owing to concerns about the gangs in the neighborhood. A sibling of one student asked the observer whether that observer was a pimp.

Anita Terry endured a most traumatic family event that resulted in the placement of Anita and her sister with their grandmother. Juan Luis Martienez witnessed an equally traumatic event involving his mother. Juan Luis was separated from his father, who was not in a position financially to care for his children, and then endured the separation from his younger siblings. The Villar brothers watched as their brother's health deteriorated, and he finally passed away. Another child was asked to care for her newborn sibling with whom she slept on the floor. A grandmother worried aloud to the Family Focus staff person about how she could pay for electricity and gas to heat the home and cook the food.

All of this is either directly or indirectly related to poverty, and while I have observed a number of poor children who have done well in school, I have rarely seen them face the obstacles faced by a number of the children involved with this research. Three of the children were being raised by their grandmothers, women who may well lack the energy and focus to be involved in child development. A fourth, Jason Green, was living with his mother in his grandmother's home. Several of the children were literally "starving for attention," and when they received that attention they performed better despite the reality that the changes needed in the home environment were often not made. None of the poor black students, and only one of the poor Latino students had their fathers in the home. Not only did this require the mothers and grand-mothers to work in most cases, but it also deprived the children of the presence of an adult male.

This meant not just the lack of the male role model, but also less time and energy for child development. While I have found this to be fairly common among poor black families (Sampson, 2002), I have also found it to be relatively uncommon among poor Latino families (Sampson, 2003). So, we have several cases of very unstable homes, several trau-matic events that affected the students, children needing attention so badly that some would do almost anything to obtain that attention, and children being raised by their grandparents. While students have been known to thrive under these conditions, it is rare.

In America, we do not like to discuss social class openly, and we do not like the notion of trying to change families. The discussion of social class often implies that one class is somehow better than another, and in a supposedly egalitarian society this is frowned upon. While I do not at all believe that one class is inherently better than another, it is clear that many of the values and beliefs and some of the behavior generally asso-ciated with the middle class is highly prized in public schools. Thus, my argument that what I term middle-class behavior helps children do bet-ter in school, and that many, if not most, poor children, especially non-white, would benefit were they to behave and believe like middle-class folks.

It is not clear that we were able to successfully assist all of the fami-lies studied to adopt many of the characteristics of the middle class as-sociated with school success. It is clear, however, that many of these families faced obstacles that make school success a low priority, even though the adults in the families very much want that success for their children or grandchildren. These obstacles would need to be overcome probably before we could assist the families with changes in their ap-proach to parenting and changes in their home environments, and that is a job for our society. It is true, however, that for the most part these families appear to concentrate upon their survival and not upon school preparation or child development, even though we devoted a year and a half to observing them and trying to help them make the needed changes.

A number of variables help determine academic success, including class size, the availability of quality preschool education, the home environment of the student, and the school-related parenting skills and behavior of the parents. While some might add the quality of teachers to this list, I have been consistently reluctant to do so, especially given that I am not clear just what that means or how this quality would be measured. It is also clear that racism and economic inequality limit the opportunities of many poor nonwhite children to do well in school, though they do not appear to hinder others.

I do not expect that racism or inequality will disappear soon, though I do believe that we should work all of the time to make this happen. I am not confident that this society will soon devote the required resources to desparately needed reductions in class size. Nor will there be the addition of enough preschool seats to help many of the children in need. It then makes sense in my view for us to focus more attention on helping parents and grandparents to develop the mind-set, attitudes, and skills that might help them better prepare their children and grandchildren for school. Work should be done on schools and with parents, and while my research focuses on the parent and family side of the issue, I do not believe that we should ignore the changes in schools that would help these children do better.

It may be that we need to consider changes in schools that might help poor nonwhite children who are being raised in a non–middle-class manner to perform better in school. That is, instead of changing parenting or child rearing, perhaps we should change the schools that teach the children who are not raised in what I would call a middle-class manner, though, as Tough (2006) correctly points out, "It is not yet entirely clear what that [school] system might look like" (77). While this is an interesting idea, I do not believe that it is really practical given that public schools prepare students for a middle-class society, and are instruments of that society. Students must therefore be trained and educated by those schools to play roles in that society, and schools that fail to do that will fail to prepare children for those roles. Even Irving (1990), who is a strong supporter of changes in school practices that might help black students perform better, acknowledges that many black parents need to be taught parenting skills that will allow them to make changes in their homes that will positively affect their children's school performance.

It is not either schools or parents/homes. It needs to be both, but at this time almost all of the attention is paid to schools. That is a mistake. It would also be a mistake to believe that all middle-income parents consistently do the things discussed in this work and by others such as Lareau (2003), Clark (1983), Comer (1993), Tapia (2000), and Bempechat (1998). As Ogbu (2003) suggests, not all middle-income parents behave like middle-class parents. Many are too busy being middle-income, and others are too self-absorbed to pay much attention to the development of their children. As I have indicated several times, where child rearing is concerned, some poor nonwhite parents do in fact behave more like most middle-class parents.

My effort to determine the efficacy of helping poor nonwhite parents and grandparents who do not behave this way to change so that they could better help their children and grandchildren to do better in school yielded mixed results. I must point out as well that this kind of approach to helping poor parents to help their children may well not be very practical. Spending the kind of time in the homes of these families that we were able to spend is costly and very time consuming, and it is unlikely that big city school systems have the time or resources to do this even if they wanted to. Some of the teaching of the parents could be done in groups to save time and money, and the curricula would need to be less detailed and individualized if a large number of families were involved. While I believe that the detailed and tailored approach is the best, it takes a long time and would cost a lot. Some compromises would need to take place.

I do believe, however, that we cannot continue in this society to compromise the help that many poor nonwhite families need if they are to help the schools do a better job with their children. That is, if they are to change to behave more like the parents of academically successful children. We may change the approach to be more practical, but we must offer that help systematically.

Appendix

SAMPLE CURRICULUM AND INTERVENTION NOTES

As I have indicated in the body of this book, a curriculum was developed for each of the eight students on the basis of the first set of observations, the response to those observations, and my subsequent analysis by various staff members from Family Focus. I have included two sample curricula—one used with one of the students from Evanston and one from the poor Latino students living in Chicago—along with samples of the notes written by staff assigned to work and intervene with the families. The notes are presented here as written with no editing on my part, but the names of the students, family members, and staff persons have been altered as they were in the body of the book.

I believe that these documents may help readers better understand what was done and how we did the work with the families.

IMPLEMENTATION DOCUMENTATION FOR SAMPSON PROJECT

Definition of Curriculum

Curriculums (Individual Family Support Plan) used with Family Focus participants should reflect Family Support principles and include:

- specific goals and objectives
- appropriate activities or interventions that support obtaining specified goals and objectives
- a system for documenting participant/family (student, parents, and other household members) progress toward accomplishment of goals and objectives.

JASON GREEN

Goal/Objective	Activities/Interventions	Timeline	Responsibility	Progress Measurement
Assist family in supporting Jason's efforts to improve grades.	Identify a quiet, organized, well-lighted space for Jason to do homework.	March 2005	Mother, Jason, and staff person	Jason will have a space to complete homework that is free of distractions and is well organized and well lit.
	Jason will do homework at 30-minute intervals.	3rd marking period	Jason	Jason will develop increased capacity to focus on schoolwork. There will be an increase of one letter grade on progress report.
	Develop a school calendar of all scheduled parent meetings, staffing, and conferences.	April 11, 2000	Staff person and Mother	Mother will have increased contact with school personnel and be more informed about events at school.

Goal/Objective	Activities/Interventions	Timeline	Responsibility	Progress Measurement
Assist family in supporting Jason's efforts to improve grades (cont.)	Jason will be referred to the 21st Century Program for one-on-one tutoring.	April 2005 (ongoing)	Staff person	Improved grades.
	Jason will spend 2–3 days at the library to complete the research project.	3rd marking period	Jason and Mother	Project will be completed on time.
Jason's needs as defined by the IEP will be more effectively addressed.	Staff person will accompany Mother to next IEP staffing.	Next IEP staffing (school will schedule)	Staff person, Mother Staff	Jason will receive more effective special education services.
	Family will be referred to the Family Resource Coalition.	April 2005		Mother will be better informed about Jason's rights as a child with a disability. Mother and Jason will have the opportunity to meet and network with other families who have a child with a disability.

Name of Student: Jason Green
Date of Visit: February 24, 2005
Beginning Time: 6:30 p.m.
Ending Time: 7:45 p.m.
Location: home
Staff Signature: _____

Type of Intervention

[X] Home Visit
[ ] After-School Programming

☐ Recreational Group Setting
☐ Parenting Group
☐ Tutoring/Mentoring
☐ Other: _____

Who Was Present?

☒ Student
☐ Mother
☐ Father
☐ Sibling
☒ Grandmother
☐ Grandfather
☐ Teacher
☐ Other: _____

Describe interactions during intervention:

(Please add additional sheets if necessary)

I arrived at Jason's house to find that his mother was not available she was at work. My observation was with grandma. Grandma and mom are two totally different people. I observed this right away. She immediately asked how his day was, and if he had homework or did he finish his homework, which I thought was great! Grandma stated that she may not always know how to help Jason but she always wanted to know if he had homework or not. Grandma was just getting home from work herself, She sat down for a while watch TV (the news), put on some gospel music and started dinner. She was concerned that her oldest grandchild had not made it in the house yet. Jason is a very quiet and shy individual and was uncomfortable asking me for help. After getting past all that, I asked him to read to me, we struggled so much with this assignment, because he cannot read and was very embarrassed about it. I told him I would bring him some easier books to start off with; I asked what type of books he enjoys reading or even learning about. He wants books on art, which I found out that he has a lot of potential if guided in the right direction. He perks up when he talks about art. Jason has very low self-esteem but through his interest in art this could be a new beginning for coming out of his overly protective shell. Jason likes school but would rather draw then go. He was not focused on his homework the whole time I was there, he found other things to talk about, including showing me his art drawings, and he wanted to watch TV. Grandma wanted Jason to stay focused and get the work done. She clearly had rules before any TV was to be watched. Jason had an assignment that needed to be done on the computer; I must add that he knows how to get around on the different programs on the computer. I was very impressed. I needed to observe his mother so it was very difficult to see what the previous observer observed. I do know that I've known the participant's mother since junior high school. She is a very caring and sweet person. She cares a lot about her children. She cares about their futures, she wants them to have a "good" education and finish school. She doesn't expect college. If it happens fine but she indicated that college isn't for everyone. Mom had a lot of issues in the school system and in her personal life that is clearly coming across to her children.

Grandma's interaction with her grandchildren is great!

Name of Student: Jason Green
Date of Visit: April 1, 2005
Beginning Time: 6:30 p.m.
Ending Time: 7:50 p.m.
Location: Home
Staff Signature: _____

Type of Intervention

[X] Home Visit
[ ] After-School Programming
[ ] Recreational Group Setting
[ ] Parenting Group
[ ] Tutoring/Mentoring
[ ] Other: _____

Who Was Present?

☒ Student
☐ Mother
☐ Father
☒ Sibling
☐ Grandmother
☐ Grandfather
☐ Teacher
☒ Other: Babysitter

Describe interactions during intervention:

(Please add additional sheets if necessary)

Jason and his family have moved to another apartment, a much bigger place. Once again Jason's mom and this time grandmother had to work late. There was a babysitter at the home when I arrived. The babysitter was given prior notice of my arrival so she knew to expect me. The babysitter's name was Sheila; she was a close friend of the family and was a consistent person that would always be there when the kids get home from school. She appeared to be very compassionate and caring towards the kids.

Jason appeared to be very withdrawn and upset about something. I started feeling that he was upset about me coming to his home. That maybe he didn't want me to come over. Before I started second guessing Jason's feelings I decided to ask him what the problem was, he responded that he was just tired. Maybe this was indeed true, because the family had been working on their apartment, moving things around getting all settled after the move. In this move we've taken a few steps back as far as having a space for Jason to do his homework. Later the babysitter and I cleaned a space for him to do his homework. I would have rather observed his mom creating a space for him but at this time mom was not available. I sat in the kitchen as I observed Jason and Sheila struggle with his homework; I was trying very hard not to be the tutor because this was not why I was here. After watching Jason struggle for 20 minutes I decided to assist Jason with his math homework. I also gave him some tools to assist him understand multiplication facts. After finishing the math homework as promised at our last home visit I brought Jason some books that he and his mom could read together. I told him he must record on the graph that I gave him each time he read with his mother. He should do this every night for 15–20 minutes. This was a major accomplishment, getting Jason some books that he would enjoy reading with his mom. On our next visit I will bring a tape recorder so that Jason could practice reading out loud and listening to him read. The goal to increase Jason's reading and math scores would only be enhanced by these techniques.

My visit with Jason was over at 7:50 p.m. as I was sitting in my car writing a few notes mom arrived at 8:03 p.m. I spoke to her briefly to let her know that I really needed her to be home during my next visit. She agreed to being home the next time. Our next visit per mom's availability will be May 19, 2005.

Goal/Objective: To increase math and reading scores

Describe progress toward accomplishment of goal(s) identified for this family: Math is still a struggle for Jason; he is making very little progress. Reading with a tape recorder will indeed increase Jason's reading levels and comprehension. I will conduct a reading fluency to assess Jason's reading grade level.

Update on school performance: Jason is registered in the 21st Century program. He adjusted well, but misses being at the center. I have developed a contact at Kingsley and will have updates on his progress monthly. Mom will get 3rd quarter grades to me as soon as possible.

Name of Student: Jason Green
Date of Visit: May 25, 2005
Beginning Time: 6:00 p.m.
Ending Time: 8:00 p.m.
Location: Kingsley School/21st Century Program and home
Staff Signature: _____

Type of Intervention

[X] Home Visit
[X] After-School Programming
[ ] Recreational Group Setting

☐ Parenting Group
☐ Tutoring/Mentoring
☐ Other: _____

Who Was Present?

☒ Student
☒ Mother
☐ Father
☒ Sibling
☐ Grandmother
☐ Grandfather
☒ Teacher
☐ Other: _____

Describe interactions during intervention:

(Please add additional sheets if necessary)

I had the opportunity to attend the 21st Century family night with Jason and his mom. My observation was one of puzzlement; mom had a chance to sit with her son in a more structured family like setting. Mom decided to visit with her friends. I spoke to mom at my last visit on how important it is to spend that alone time with her son. I wanted her to inquire about his day, ask about his school work, even if she doesn't have a clue on what it was about, which most of the time she doesn't. Jason's social skills are very low, he's a loner and very quiet at times. He has although made little improvements in his grades. Jason needs a lot of assistance with his writing skills. I purchased a handwriting workbook for Jason to work on for the summer. He is to work on two pages a day.

Mom still has not found a stable job but is still looking, especially since she moved she needs to secure a job to keep her apartment. I also observed that mom gives a lot more attention to baby and not to Jason. This next statement is my opinion only, but I feel that the reason Jason does not try harder in school because he is trying to get attention from mom in any way. He wants her to ask about his day, he wants her to sit down with him and help with his homework or just to have some alone time with just him. Don't get me wrong she loves her son I can clearly see this,

Jason just want some alone time with her. He has the potential to be a bright child in all subjects with *assistance*. Jason will continue to work on his academic journal this summer; he will also be enrolled in the 21st Century Summer Reading Intensive Program. To ensure his academic excellence he will re-enroll in the 21st Century project in the fall. I have also given Jason a tape recorder so that he can start reading and listening to himself read. Last but not least Jason will also be given a writing tablet that will assist and enhance his writing skills. As I suggested to Mom, Jason needs to take this summer and really work on the skills I have mentioned, especially since he will be entering 5th grade he needs to be prepared. And she needs to play a major role in this preparation process. She must give him uninterrupted time, even its only 30 min. a day. This would be a major accomplishment this summer for Jason and his Mom.

Goal/Objective: To improve reading and writing skills.

Describe progress toward accomplishment of goal(s) identified for this family: Progress is slow but the family has agreed to follow recommendations mentioned to ensure success. These recommendations include the academic journal, writing workbook, and reading grade-level books with assistance from his mother and the 21st Century staff.

Update on School Performance: Report card indicates that Jason still has work to do to increase his grades in writing, reading, and math skills.

FEDERICO AND JOSE LUIS VILLAR

Goal/Objective	Activities/Interventions	Timeline	Responsibility	Progress Measurement
Provide parents with support in assuming increased responsibility for boys' education.	1. Explore with parents their interest in participating in parenting classes (keeping in mind that they have already raised quite a few	Week of April 5th	Parents and Outreach worker	Parents will be participants in parenting class.

(continued)

Goal/Objective	Activities/Interventions	Timeline	Responsibility	Progress Measurement
Provide parents with support in assuming increased responsibility for boys' education. (cont.)	children and may not be open to this suggestion). If there is an interest, make appropriate referral. If not, parents may be responsive to other methods of "parenting education," such as videos or printed material that can be shared with them.			
	2. Set standards and rules in the household that will govern "homework" time, i.e. no television or music while any of the children are doing homework.	Week of April 5	Parents, Federico and Jose Luis, Outreach worker	The household will be respectful of children's homework time.
	3. Provide the Villars with verbal support during home visits for interest and involvement in sons' schoolwork.	April 2005 (ongoing)	Outreach worker	Parents will begin to exhibit increased interest in boys' homework.
	4. Model appropriate behavior for involvement with sons' schoolwork and for acknowledging positive behaviors.	April 2005 (ongoing)	Outreach worker	Parents will have increased awareness of sons' positive homework "behaviors."
	5. Encourage parent participation in	June–August 2005	Outreach worker	

Goal/Objective	Activities/Interventions	Timeline	Responsibility	Progress Measurement
Provide parents with support in assuming increased responsibility for boys' education. (cont.)	LSC or other parent group at their sons' school. They may welcome the opportunity to befriend or mentor younger parents. This may be a goal for the beginning of the 2005–2006 school year.			

Goal/Objective	Activities/Interventions	Timeline	Responsibility	Progress Measurement
Provide both boys with opportunities to promote increased confidence and self-esteem.	1. Explore possibility of boys becoming involved in extracurricular activities. Their school and church may offer possibilities. Perhaps there is a band, choir, sports team that the boys may be interested in and can join. In consideration of the "bullying" mentioned, parents and boys may be interested in	April 2005 (ongoing)	Parents and Outreach worker	The boys will have some constructive activities in their lives.

(continued)

Goal/Objective	Activities/Interventions	Timeline	Responsibility	Progress Measurement
Provide both boys with opportunities to promote increased confidence and self-esteem. (*cont.*)	them participating in an activity that will build physical strength and make them better equipped to defend themselves.			
	2. Assist family in practicing complimenting one another. Outreach worker can model this behavior during home visits.	April 2005 (ongoing)	Outreach worker	All family members will begin to feel increased feelings of self-worth. There may be an increase in outward demonstrations of affection.
	3. Encourage parents to assess their sleeping arrangements. Help them to develop new sleeping arrangements in the house. It is noted that Fernando and Jose Luis share a bedroom and perhaps a bed with their parents.*	April 2005	Outreach worker, Parents	The boys will not be sleeping with their parents.
	4. Assist parents and boys in identifying household chores the boys will have responsibility for, such as emptying	April 2005	Parents, Federico and Jose Luis, and Outreach worker	Increased sense of responsibility and capability

Goal/Objective	Activities/Interventions	Timeline	Responsibility	Progress Measurement
Provide both boys with opportunities to promote increased confidence and self-esteem. (cont.)	trash and sweeping floors. Rules governing the chores should be developed; such as how often task is accomplished, by whom, etc.			

*This situation is potentially troublesome. As noted in the material provided by Dr. Sampson, staff should keep an eye out for any indications that something is amiss.

Goal/Objective	Activities/Interventions	Timeline	Responsibility	Progress Measurement
Implement strategies to improve English, reading, and writing skills.	1. Refer Jose Luis and Federico to 21st Century Program.	April 2005 (ongoing)	Outreach worker, 21st Century staff, Parents	Jose Luis and Federico will demonstrate increased interest in English, reading, and writing.
	2. Encourage parents to communicate regularly with 21st Century staff who work with their children. 21st Century staff can make recommendations /suggestions on ways that parents can help with homework.	April 2005 (ongoing)	Outreach worker, 21st Century staff, Parents	Improvement in grades.
	3. 21st Century staff provides activities and resources to encourage literacy with Jose Luis and Federico.	April 2005 (ongoing)	Outreach worker, 21st Century staff, Parents	

February 15, 2005 (home visit)

Goal/Objective: Propose the continuation of the DePaul Project and curriculum/contract.

Describe interactions during intervention: The family opened the door for the home visit. We reviewed and discussed the goals and objectives of the curriculum and the contract. Their reaction was positive and enthusiastic. Federico was accepting and seemed very eager to continue in the project and to know they will receive more support to help him succeed in school.

Describe progress toward accomplishment of goal(s) identified for this family: We sat in the dining room and identified a place to do homework quietly and study without interruptions. Mother and son felt supported and Mother responded that she would put more effort into supporting her children. She agreed to participate in the English as a Second Language (ESL) class to help her children. They came to the Center to enroll in the ESL class.

Update on school progress: Mrs. Sanchez (mother) plans to visit son's classroom to talk to teacher.

March 2, 2005 (home visit)

Goal/Objective: Review curriculum and sign contract.

Describe interactions during intervention: Curriculum was described and Mrs. Sanchez realized how important it is to keep in touch with son's teacher and get feedback from her. Fernando is taking his responsibility seriously and is committed to making changes in his performance. He wants to see good results and he's changing habits to improve. Mrs. Sanchez is supportive where she can be. She has older children who have been enlisted to help when she can't. Federico was doing his homework and Mrs. Sanchez called him to review the curriculum with him. Federico reacted positively and signed the contract. Mother explained that this was a very important promise.

Describe progress toward accomplishment of goal(s) identified for this family: Federico has decided to not get interrupted while doing his homework in his room. He remains in his room until his homework is completed. He doesn't watch too much television and goes to bed on time.

Update on school progress: Federico received an award for his outstanding progress during the month of February.

April 13, 2006 (home visit)
Mrs. Sanchez states that Federico is doing better. Mrs. Sanchez met with Federico's teacher last week and she told Mrs. Sanchez that Federico is showing significant improvement and does not need to enroll in extra activities.

May 12, 2005 (home visit)
Mrs. Sanchez said that Federico is doing well in school and that there are no problems with his homework and his grades are improved. Federico was not home today. It seems like Federico is not participating in the program any more.

June 16, 2005 (home visit)
Today Federico and I practiced the multiplication table. He needs to practice tables for 7, 8, and 9. He also read a story and wrote a few paragraphs, which he did well. He is happy because his teacher told him that he passed to the next grade. His teacher said he is doing well in school and will be attending summer school.

Mr. and Mrs. Sanchez's Responsibilities

1. Make sure Federico has a place to do homework that is quiet, well-lit, and organized.
2. Make sure that the TV, video games, radio, etc. are turned off while they are doing their homework.
3. Make sure that there is a designated time for Jose Luis and Federico to do their homework.
4. Make sure that there are consequences for not doing homework, such as no television for one night.
5. Reward positive behaviors.

Federico's Responsibilities

1. Bring home assignments, textbooks, and anything else needed to complete your homework.
2. Make sure that you understand the assignments.
3. Ask an adult for help if you need it.
4. Turn you homework in on time

5. Do not turn on videos, TV, and games while you are doing your homework.

6. Show your homework to your mother or one of your grandparents when you finish it.

BIBLIOGRAPHY

WORKS CITED

Bempechat, A. W. (1998). *Against the odds: How "at risk" children exceed expectations*. San Francisco: Jossey-Bass.

Clark, R. M. (1983). *Family life and school achievement: Why poor black children succeed or fail*. Chicago: University of Chicago Press.

Comer, J. P. (1993). Inner-city education: A theoretical and intervention model. In W. J. Wilson (Ed.), *Sociology and the public agenda*, 300–315. Newbury Park, CA: Sage.

Constantino, S. M. (2003). *Engaging all families: Creating a positive school culture by putting research into practice*. Lanham, MD: Scarecrow Education.

Dyson, M. E. (2005, June, July). An Afristocrat in winter. Excerpt from *Is Bill Cosby right? Or has the black middle class lost its mind? Savoy Magazine* 1(4), 68–72.

Dyson, M. E. (2005). *Is Bill Cosby right? Or has the black middle class lost its mind?* Philadelphia, PA: Basic Books.

Entwisle, D. R., Alexander, K. L., & Olson, L. S. (1997). *Children, schools, and inequality*. Boulder, CO: Westview.

Epstein, J., Samders, M. G., Simon, B. S., Salinas, K. C., Jansorn, N. R., & Van Voorhis, F. L. (2002). *School, family, and community partnerships: Your handbook for action* (2nd ed.). Thousand Oaks, CA: Corwin.

Ford, D. (1993). Black students' achievement orientation as a function of perceived family achievement orientation and demographic variables. *Journal of Negro Education, 62*(1), 47–64.

Fordham, S. & Ogbu, J. U. (1986). Black students' school success: coping with the burden of "acting white." *Urban Review 18*(3), 1–31.

Furstenberg, F. F., Jr., Cook, T. D., Eccles, J., Elder, G. H., Jr., & Sameroff, A. (1999). *Managing to make it: Urban families and adolescent success.* Chicago: University of Chicago Press.

Henderson, A. T., & Berla, N. (Eds.). (1994). *A new generation of evidence: The family is critical to student achievement.* Washington, DC: Center for Law and Education.

Herrnstein, R. J., & Murray, C. (1994). *The bell curve: Intelligence and class structure in American life.* New York: Free Press.

Howell, W. G., & Peterson, P. E. (2002). *The education gap: Vouchers and urban schools.* Washington, DC: Brookings Institution Press.

Irving, J. I. (1990). *Black students and school failure: Policies, practices, and prescriptions.* Westport, CN: Praeger.

Jensen, A. (1969). How much can we boost I.Q. and scholastic achievement? *Harvard Educational Review, 2,* 1–123. [Reprint series]

Lareau, A. (2000). *Home advantage: Social class and parental intervention in elementary education.* Lanham, MD: Rowman & Littlefield.

Lareau, A. (2003). *Unequal childhoods: Class, race, and family life.* Berkeley, CA: University of California Press.

Mickelson, R. A. (1998). *A report to the U.S. District Court for the Western District of North Carolina in the case of* Capacechione v. Charlotte-Mecklenburg Schools et al. Unpublished manuscript.

Murphy, J. C. (2003). Case studies in African-American school success and parenting behaviors. *Young Children 58*(6), 85–89.

Ogbu, J. (1978). *Minority education and caste: The American system in cross-cultural perspective.* New York: Academic Press.

Ogbu, J. (2003). *Black American students in an affluent suburb: A study of academic disengagement.* Philadelphia, PA: Basic Books.

Sampson, W. A. (2002). *Black student achievement: How much do family and school really matter?* Lanham, MD: Scarecrow.

Sampson, W. A. (2003). *Poor Latino families and school preparation: Are they doing the right things?* Lanham, MD: Scarecrow Education.

Sampson, W. A. (2004). *Black and brown: Race, ethnicity, and school preparation.* Lanham, MD: Scarecrow Education.

Tapia, J. (2000). Schooling and learning in U.S.-Mexican American families: A case study of households. *Urban Review, 32*(1), 25–44.

Tough, P. (2006, November 26). Still left behind: What will it really take to close the education gap. *New York Times Magazine*, 44–77.

Trueba, H. (1988). Culturally based explanations of minority students' academic achievement. *Anthropology and Education Quarterly, 19,* 270–285.

ADDITIONAL SOURCES

Brooks-Gunn, J. (1995). Strategies for altering the outcomes of poor children and their families. In P. L. C. Landsdale & J. B. Gunn (Eds.), *Escape from poverty: What makes a difference for children?* Cambridge: Cambridge University Press.

Coleman, J. S. (1981). *The adolescent society.* Westport, CT: Greenwood.

Coleman, J. S. (1991). *Policy perspectives: Parental involvement in education.* Washington, DC: Office of Educational Research and Improvement, U.S. Department of Education.

Comer, J. P. (1980). *School power: Implications of an intervention project.* New York: Free Press.

Constantino, S. M. (2003). *Engaging all families: Creating a positive school culture by putting research into practice.* Lanham, MD: Scarecrow Education.

Delgado-Gaitan, C. (1992). School matters in the Mexican-American home: Socializing children to education. *American Educational Research Journal, 29(3),* 495–513.

Gutman, L. M., & Mc Lloyd, V. C. (2000). Parents' management of their children's education within the home, at school, and in the community: An examination of African-American families living in poverty. *The Urban Review, 32(1),* 1–24.

Hu, A. (1997). Education and race: The performance of minority students in affluent areas refutes the prevailing educational shibboleths. *National Review, 49(17),* 52–56.

Illinois Board of Education. (2005). *Illinois district report card.* Springfield, IL: Illinois Board of Education.

Kozol, Jonathon. (1992). *Savage inequalities: Children in America's schools.* New York: Harper-Collins.

Lipset, S., & Bendix, R. (1959). *Social mobility in industrial society.* Berkeley: University of California Press.

Mackler, B (1971). Blacks who are academically successful. *Urban Education, 5,* 210–237.

McAdoo, H. P., & McAdoo, J. L. (1985). *Black children: Social, educational and parental environments.* Beverly Hills, CA: Sage.

McWhorter, J. H. (2000). *Losing the race: Self sabotage in black America.* New York: Free Press.

Neisser, U. (1986). *The school achievement of minority children.* Hillsdale, NJ: Erlbaum.

Phares, E. J. (1976). *Locus of control in personality.* Morristown, NJ: General Learning Press.

Reynolds, A. J., & Gill, S. (1994). The role of parental perspectives in the school adjustment of inner city black children. *Journal of Youth and Adolescence, 23,* 671–693.

Rist, R. (1970). Student social class and teacher expectations: The self-fulfilling prophecy in ghetto education. *Harvard Educational Review, 40,* 411–451.

Steinberg, L. (1996). *Beyond the classroom: Why school reform has failed and what parents need to do.* New York: Simon and Schuster.

U.S. Department of Commerce, Bureau of the Census. (2000). *2000 census of the population and housing: Summary of the population and housing characteristics.* Washington, DC: Author.

West, C. (1993). *Race matters.* Boston: Beacon.

INDEX

ABOUT THE AUTHOR

William Alfred Sampson is a professor of public policy at DePaul University in Chicago. His research has focused on both social class and the education of poor nonwhite students, bringing together social class variables and education issues. He has studied the relationship between academic achievement and the family dynamic of poor nonwhite students for the past nine years, arguing that, based upon data, some poor nonwhite students manage to perform quite well in school, while others in the same communities, and often in the same schools, perform poorly. The explanation for the difference in performance, according to Dr. Sampson and a number of other scholars, is not the income level or the school. Rather, it is the ability of some poor nonwhite families to adopt the values, beliefs, attitudes, and much of the behavior, of middle-income families. Dr. Sampson argues that the focus of the debate over the gap in school performance between some poor nonwhite students and most middle-income white students is not the school, but the family.